PAUL EVANS was born in Limavady and educa. ... Ballymena Academy and Stranmillis College. Several years as a teacher convinced him that real work was overrated and he joined the BBC in Belfast as a radio producer. In his eventual role as head of production for BBC Northern Ireland, he was executive producer of television entertainment output that included Gerry Anderson, Patrick Kielty and The Hole in the Wall Gang, as well as series presented by Hugo Duncan – *Town Challenge* and *Hugo and Friends*. He continues to produce radio and television programmes but only if they allow him enough time to engage in his two other pastimes: playing weekend gigs with Hooker – an ageing but suitably noisy rock band – and searching for the perfect pint of Guinness, not necessarily in that order.

UNCLE HUGO

THE STORY OF THE WEE MAN FROM STRABANE

Paul Evans

BLACKSTAFF
PRESS
BELFAST

First published in 2008 by
Blackstaff Press
4c Heron Wharf, Sydenham Business Park
Belfast, BT3 9LE

© Text, Paul Evans, 2008
© Photographs, Hugo Duncan, 2008, except where otherwise indicated

Paul Evans has identified his right under the
Copyright, Designs and Patents Act 1988 to be identified as the author of this work.

Typeset by IMD Typesetting & Design

Printed in Wales by Creative Print & Design

A CIP catalogue record for this book is available from the
British Library

ISBN 978-0-85640-820-5

www.blackstaffpress.com

Contents

Preface   vii

Is Everybody Happy?   1

Wee Susie   17

The Three-Chord Trick   37

A Wedding and a Funeral   53

What Comes Around   69

The Tall Men   83

Playing by Night and Pubbing by Day   95

Second Chance   109

Turn Your Radio On   121

Don't Give Up the Night Job   133

Remember, Your Uncle Hugo Loves You   145

That's Me, On the TV   157

Preface

I have known Hugo Duncan for nearly two decades. For ten of those years, during my previous life with BBC Northern Ireland, he bombarded me with tapes, videos and handwritten notes as a reminder that he was a broadcasting event waiting to happen. And he was right. In 1998 I was part of a small group that brought Hugo to the early afternoon slot on Radio Ulster to present a programme that is unique to this country.

What intrigues me about Hugo's phenomenal success is not the music, for I am not an Irish country fan, but rather the connection he makes as a performer and broadcaster with hundreds of thousands of people from all backgrounds and walks of life in Northern Ireland and beyond. They clearly recognise him as one of their own, a kindred spirit, for his achievements would be nothing without their support. This book, then, is not an attempt to explain the world of country and Irish music. What I've tried to do is unravel the secret of Hugo's special gift – how he engages so easily with his people. And, for his legions of devoted fans who love him, I've drawn together some of the highs and lows of the fifty-eight years that make up his colourful and extraordinary life.

Hugo and I are indebted to Patsy Horton at Blackstaff Press, who has had such faith in this project, and Hilary Bell, who helped bring order to the story. I'd like also to thank Anne Tannahill for her advice when the book was just a notion.

I've enjoyed many hours with Hugo chatting about his life, and my thanks are due also to his wife, Joan, whose recollections informed so much of that discussion.

My final thanks are to my family – Joanne, Rebecca and Matt – who must feel as if they have lived with their Uncle Hugo for the past year.

Paul Evans

1

Is Everybody Happy?

Monday 17 March 2008 is cold but sunny across Northern Ireland. Given that the previous weeks saw the tail end of high winds and rain from the North Atlantic, for hundreds of organising committees, there couldn't be more perfect weather for the parades, carnivals and sporting occasions traditionally held on Saint Patrick's Day.

At around twelve thirty, Hugo Duncan is patrolling the carvery restaurant in Joe Mahon's Hotel in Irvinestown. Every now and then he dips a spoon into the dish he is carrying and eats with gusto. The bowl contains two scoops of chocolate ice cream and a couple more of vanilla, on top of a square of chocolate sponge, plus some whipped cream on the side. Hugo has a grin from ear to ear. 'Breakfast,' he announces happily, as he helps himself to another spoonful of ice cream.

Among the many events held to celebrate the 2008 Saint Patrick's Day is the first outside broadcast of the year for Hugo's programme on BBC Radio Ulster, *Country Afternoon*. By the end of 2008 he will have taken his show to over forty venues across Northern Ireland, and a few beyond, if he can persuade those in charge of the purse strings to release a bit of spare cash. He's received dozens of invitations to bring the afternoon show to different Saint Patrick's Day events, and having considered them all, he and his producer, Joanne Murphy – known to listeners as the Wee Woman with the Big Stick – have decided to put on their own special concert at Mahon's Hotel.

Which is why Hugo is patrolling the restaurant; he is the host today and he's supervising lunch for his guests. Quietly pointing out to the cashier which of those in the queue belong to his party, he encourages Conal Gallen to horse a bit more pavlova into him; the Donegal comedian has attained cult status ever since his agricultural love song, 'Horse It into Ya, Cynthia', became the most requested song on *Country Afternoon*. Hugo assures nervous autograph-hunters that Foster and Allen, the Irish traditional duo, won't mind in the slightest interrupting their lunch to pose for photographs – and he's right. He ushers Elaine Boyle to a table in the manner of a proud father leading his daughter up the aisle. And why wouldn't he? In her white petticoat dress decorated with bright green shamrocks, the young Donegal singer is as fresh as the day outside and Hugo knows rightly that no matter how well known he is, he always looks better alongside a pretty girl.

And all the time he's greeting his flock, waving, calling out names, hugging old friends, exchanging banter and having a quiet word with anyone who seems in need of a bit of comfort.

As he glances out the window to the main street, he sees a bright red Reliant Robin pulling up at the front door of the hotel. This is no ordinary vehicle, for the owner has had a custom paint job done on it: along one side, it advertises the hotel's daily carvery; Maginty's Goat is painted on the front; and, on both doors of this three-wheel car, are words that will be familiar to any of Hugo's many listeners: 'Uncle Hugo Loves You, Ye Will, Ye Will, Ye Will'. The driver too has had a bit of a custom job done, for, presumably in recognition of the day that's in it, he is sporting a tartan bonnet on top of a bright red wig that looks as if it's made out of tufts of hair left over from the clippings of an Irish red setter.

In the queue for the carvery is Paddy Bradley and the boy in the chef's hat with the carving knife gets a special nod from Hugo. Paddy is one of those who has stuck by Hugo through the good days and the bad; who has, in so many ways, helped him in his business for nigh on forty years. Today he's just along for the crack, and Hugo makes sure that his old friend is treated to an extra slice of the roast of the day.

And that is what is at the heart of this afternoon's broadcast – old friends. Everyone involved today feels comfortable in each other's company; they are relaxed, there's no tension or pressure in the air, not even for the BBC staff who are in charge of an hour and a half's live radio. Above all, performers, audience, hotel staff, producers and sound engineers know why they're gathering in Joe Mahon's function hall. It's a special holiday, they're in the heart of rural Ulster and their friend Hugo Duncan knows what music entertainment is all about. So he should – he's been doing it for nearly half a century.

The sound crew declare the lunch to have been the best they've had on an outside broadcast. For some reason, BBC sound men tend to be called Davy and today there are two Davys and a George who will look after the technical side of the business while Hugo does the entertaining. Having eaten their fill, Davy, Davy and George head back into the hall to their microphones, cables, two-way radios and a pair of mixing desks; one of which stands at the side of the stage and the other in the balcony. Hugo walks to the back yard of the hotel, pausing at today's car to collect his gear. Though not strictly true, he does give the impression that he has a car for every day of the week and, over his life, he's probably had a car for each year that he's been on this earth. Not bad going, considering he didn't buy his first until he was seventeen. Today he's behind the wheel of a black model with smoked glass windows.

In the back are boxes of Uncle Hugo baseball hats and mugs, as well as several six packs of Red Bull that he'll get through in the course of the afternoon. He tucks one of these under his arm, gathers up his black suit, T-shirt and shirt, and strolls through the side door of the hall.

At its peak, Mahon's dance hall regularly drew people from Tyrone, Fermanagh, Donegal, Leitrim, Cavan and beyond. Sunday entertainment didn't begin until eleven o'clock at night, so heaven knows how much work was done on a Monday morning. As the hotel has expanded and modernised, and the styles of entertainment have changed, the hall now wears a slightly weary look but it is a classic example of the venues that once stood at every vantage point across Ireland, from busy town centres to lonely crossroads that were equidistant from half a dozen villages.

The hall holds upward of five hundred. The ceiling is high, a reminder that it was originally built as a cinema. There are two glitter balls set among some crystal chandeliers, and there's a large balcony area, reached by a wide staircase from a sizeable lobby with its cloakrooms. A bar and serving hatches occupy one half of the length of the hall and the whole is dominated by a high, deep stage with its proscenium arch, backdrops and curtains. The height of the stage ensures that when the floor is packed with dancers, it is still possible to see the main act without having to peer through bodies or stand on a chair. The whole impression is of a space built for a single purpose – to provide entertainment for as many people as possible at one go.

As Hugo enters through the side door he notes that there are already a hundred people or so in the hall and he nods in satisfaction. They look lost in the cavernous space and most are sitting at the back, but it's not yet one o'clock and he's certain a few more will turn up before long. 'They'll be at home getting their lunch,' he says to himself. 'There's time enough yet.' Nevertheless, there's already a sense of anticipation and the first of the afternoon's several hundred exchanges of banter takes place.

A voice cries out, 'Hey, Hugo, come on down here and see me!' The speaker is a young man, resplendent in a green bowler hat and shiny green tie, and the decoration extends to the wheelchair.

'You come and see me!' shouts Hugo.

'I can't. I broke my leg.'

'Mother of God,' mutters Hugo with genuine interest as he danders over. 'What did you do?'

'I broke it in a car accident, on Boxing Day, in six places.'

With his arm around the shoulders of his friend in the wheelchair, Hugo addresses anyone close at hand. 'This is Davy, the best man around. Have you your pipe with you? Davy has the biggest pipe in Fermanagh.'

On cue, Davy produces a silver-bound, meerschaum-style pipe and proudly holds it aloft for all to see.

'I'll come back and see you later,' says Hugo. 'Here, do you want a drink?'

'No thanks, Hugo, I'll get a cup of tea. Did you hear the one about . . . ?'

But Hugo has scarpered before he's delayed any further.

His reputation for enjoying stories and jokes encourages fans to come up with some that he hasn't heard previously and if he stood and listened to every one, half the afternoon would have gone. It means he has to keep his ears peeled when chatting to people on air, for if he's not paying attention, he can get caught out. At one outside broadcast, he was chatting to a man while being reminded to keep an eye on the clock because the two o'clock news slot was approaching rapidly.

Hugo casually asked, 'Is the wife with you?'

'She is, aye. I'm just back from the chemist's, you know.'

At this point, an alarm bell should have gone off at the back of Hugo's mind but he was concentrating too much on the clock.

'Dear me, what's wrong with you?' he said.

'Nothing much. I was looking for Viagra and the chemist says, "Have you a prescription?" and I said no, but I had a photograph of the wife, so he looked at that and said it would be no problem.'

You never know the moment.

As Hugo heads off backstage to change, he has a word for everybody. 'Hiya, Josie. Hello, Anne, what about the wee fellow? Eileen, you'll sing for us later, ye will, ye will. There's the Solid Man from Lisburn, any woman of eighty looking for a toy boy need look no further, he's got everything a woman needs; well, of that age anyway.'

The band is playing through a couple of songs so that Davy, Davy and George can do their sound checks. Then Conal Gallen comes on stage to rehearse a verse or two of the epic, 'I'll Make Love to You in the Henhouse if You'll Only Egg Me On', at which point the punters already settled in the hall nod to one another, reassured that they're not going to be disappointed. This afternoon is going to be about fun and entertainment.

The band is dressed in dark tones, as are Conal and the other singers, Boxcar Brian, from Moira direction, and Gary Gamble, a fellow Strabane man, so, when Elaine appears for her sound check bedecked in white and green, she draws sighs of admiration from the crowd. The men pretend not to be looking but they are, until their attention is drawn elsewhere, for at ten past one there's a rattle as the shutters of the bar go up. Two men in their forties are the first to sidle up in that casual manner that suggests they had no intention of taking alcohol at all this afternoon but now that they've bumped into a bar, they might as well have a pint.

By the time that Hugo reappears at a quarter past one, there are about two hundred and fifty in the hall. He collects his microphone to start warming up the crowd and the buzz and atmosphere lift as more and more people squeeze through from the back.

'Is everybody happy?' he roars at them.

'Yes,' they roar back.

He's on the floor of the hall, shaking hands and waving, and now all the patter is relayed through the PA system as he rehearses the exchanges with his fans that will continue throughout the broadcast.

'You see this man here? He can handle three bottles of vodka, play the Lambeg drum and change nappies at the same time. Don't talk to me about your multitasking, girls.'

Someone plants a hat in the shape of a giant pint of Guinness on Hugo's head as he nods to the band, who launch into 'Amarillo'. Singing, he races across the floor to dance with a lady in a wheelchair. She is clapping her hands and singing along as he pushes her round in circles. He shoves the microphone in front of an elderly man, who, without any prompting, sings the chorus at the top of his voice.

In the last few minutes it seems as if another hundred people have come in and Hugo shouts for more chairs. Joe and his staff are already bringing them in and what was an empty dance floor at the front of the stage is now filling up rapidly with chairs and tables.

'Plenty of room at the front. Come on up,' he calls. 'All you people at the door, come away up here, sure we're all friends this Paddy's Day.' He encourages them in as 'Amarillo' swings to a close and then introduces the members of the band. 'We have Sammy on drums, Seanie on bass, Eamon on keyboards and guitar and, on piano, the lovely Ann Marie. The good-looking one at the front is me.'

All the time he bounces backwards and forwards to producer Joanne and the production assistant, Patricia Coyle, known to all as Trish, checking details and receiving words of encouragement. Then he's back in the crowd.

'Eileen's going to sing for us – give Eileen a note. What'll you sing? "There's Always a Kettle on the Boil"? Ach, ye will, ye will. Take her away, boys.'

And Eileen launches into her party piece with scant regard for the notes played by Eamon but with all the enthusiasm and joy that God has given her, because her friend Hugo has asked her to sing.

Boxcar Brian, who will perform the opening number, is introduced to the crowd as he sings a couple of bars for a final sound check before Hugo gives out last-minute instructions.

'We're going live in a couple of minutes, so here's the opening music and I want you all to sing along. Let's try it.'

The familiar jingle rings out and there's a bit of a raggle-taggle effort to do the 'la, la, la' chorus.

'I suppose it's all right, but if you could all try and do it together, it might sound a bit better. One more time, and when I shout Irvinestown, I want you all to cheer your heads off. One, two, three.'

In time-honoured fashion, he slags them for sounding as if they're at a funeral and says that he'd probably get more life out of the corpse, all of which delights them hugely. He grins, has a quick word with Joanne, climbs onto the stage, and then it's show time.

'David Dunseith's saying goodbye now. Thirty seconds to go. Remember, I want to hear everyone. Can you hear me up in the balcony? You're looking good. Here we go.'

Always fussing, he settles his black shirt collar under the suit jacket as the jingle plays.

'Welcome to Saint Patrick's Day with me, Hugo Duncan, and all my friends in Irvinestown,' says Hugo, as he leaps off his feet in his eagerness to spur on the crowd.

Before the music fades, the band licks into an Irish jig at a rate of knots that would leave Michael Flatley gasping for breath. Hugo, a medal-winning dancer himself, performs his own jig as he sings 'Skiddely, aye, dye, dye, skiddely, aye dee dye dee dye' along to the music, and without a break, he asks for a big round of applause for Boxcar as the band moves into a stomping version of the Jim Reeves classic 'Yonder Comes a Sucker'. It's not often that the words 'stomping' and Jim Reeves are mentioned in the same breath or written in the same sentence, but, in this case, it's a fair reflection of the energy that goes into Boxcar's opening song.

And they're away, up and running, for the next hour and a half of Saint Patrick's Day afternoon.

This is Hugo Duncan heartland, a few miles down the road from his home in Strabane, County Tyrone. He came from a community like this and wherever else he has travelled and performed, it is where the music he loves is rooted. He is a singer and a broadcaster of a style of musical entertainment that has never been fashionable but has never gone out of fashion. What he does on outside broadcasts is engage with the people who take joy and pleasure from his music, and this is simply an extension of what he has been doing as a touring performer for four decades.

No other radio show in Northern Ireland hosts so many programmes away from the studio and Hugo is happy to go anywhere. Not all of these broadcasts are on the scale of this Saint Patrick's Day celebration; often they take place because he knows someone who could do with a bit of special cheering up. One of the many framed photographs on Hugo's desk in the BBC shows himself and his old music friend Big Tom (of Big Tom and the Mainliners) singing a duet outside the front porch of the Ingram family home in Lisnaskea, County Fermanagh. This is a family of six adult brothers and sisters, four of whom through illness are unable to look after themselves and are cared for by their siblings, Lorna and Niall. They are all great fans of Hugo's radio show, so he took his programme to their house for an afternoon. He was accompanied by local country artists, including Big Tom, T.R. Dallas and John Glenn, who have helped and supported the family down the years. Such was the crush of well-wishers and friends that the only space left to accommodate the robust figures of Big Tom and Hugo was the porch.

Such visits are well appreciated by listeners. 'We had emails from all over the place after that programme,' Hugo recalls, 'even some from the States. People just wanted to let me know that through the programme they felt in touch with the sufferings of the Ingram family and yet at the same time were inspired to hear that there could be music and laughter and fun in that house.'

By complete contrast in terms of venue, he has broadcast from major summer festivals, such as the one at Shane's Castle in County Antrim, where there might be two thousand gathered round. He's been in old folks' homes, guested at carnivals and village fairs and stood on the streets of housing estates that represent various political and religious persuasions.

Many of the year's outside broadcasts are planned months ahead; the team pencils in the usual holiday dates plus major festivals and events that occur at roughly the same time every year. The Ould Lammas Fair in Ballycastle, County Antrim, for example, is one that will always be considered because it attracts enormous crowds and the atmosphere created by the natural crack and banter of the people is exactly the same as that in Mahon's Hotel. But not every date is booked in advance. It's easy to take the programme to popular, well-established gigs, but room is always left for small, low-key celebrations, such as the afternoon with the Ingram family, and invitations from people who perhaps don't contact Hugo till the event is almost upon them. Such invitations often come from communities that have assumed that makers of a radio programme wouldn't be bothered to come and share in their entertainment.

A member of a group that runs a day centre for elderly folk in Bangor once suggested that Hugo might join them for an afternoon. She mentioned, almost apologetically, that it would be such a lift to their spirits, and although they were all getting on in years 'quite a few of them would still be up for a bit of fun. You might even get a song or two out of them!' Joanne and Hugo seized the chance with scarcely a second's thought. The centre laid on the tea and buns; visitors were bussed in from similar associations in the area; Hugo booked two of his favourite musicians who have at their fingertips every song in his repertoire; and the place rocked, or vibrated gently at least, from lunchtime till mid-afternoon. Not only did he find folk volunteering to give him a song, Hugo also received two proposals of marriage and an offer to see him afterwards up the stairs, no questions asked. 'I always say to Joan, my wife, it's good to know I've still got it after all these years,' he laughs.

Some of these broadcasts link in with BBC initiatives such as the computer-awareness sessions delivered through the BBC Community Bus (fondly known as the Big Yellow Bus), something to which Hugo gave his enthusiastic support. As a result, the planning can become even more complex, involving, as it does other BBC departments, as well as the general public. 'I enjoy going out with the bus,' he says, 'because the people know that I know no more about computers and the Internet than they do, so they don't mind coming along if I'm there. The other reason I enjoy it is because Campbell, the bus driver, wears the same size trousers as me, so I don't look as bad as when I'm on my own.'

Joanne and Hugo share the planning, and Trish makes the phone calls to book facilities, guests and musicians, and attends to the dozens of small matters that come with taking a popular radio show on the road. Never mind the toilets, is there anywhere to get a decent cup of tea? Every venue is visited before the broadcast date to check vehicle access, local facilities, power supplies, parking, any police requirements, and where the tastiest sandwiches can be found. The most important factor to be considered is whether they have obtained the best site to maximise their presence and attract most people. Hugo makes a point of going on as many of these reconnaissance trips as he can. He is the one who has to deliver the programme from the agreed place and, if there are any potential problems, he'd rather get his spoke in a week or so in advance than on the morning of the outside broadcast itself.

If wanting to be physically among the communities of the North is the core reason why he goes on the road, live entertainment is what he delivers. There's been a long tradition on Hugo's outside broadcasts that all the music has to be live: no CDs, no pre-recorded tracks. This rule also fits in perfectly with Hugo's belief that his job is to play the music his listeners love, performed by the people they know. Every Hugo Duncan outside broadcast offers a platform for live performance and that applies equally to a new local singer with her first recordings as to a long-established Grand Ole Opry singer such as Gene Watson.

So there's a constant search for and juggling of artists to match the dates that fill up the outside broadcast diary. And it's not always a smooth process. Running a practical eye over Hugo's selection will often result in Joanne querying the proposed schedule.

'Declan Nerney's playing down in Longford the night before. Do you think it's fair to ask him to get up to Dunloy for lunchtime?'

'Ach, Declan'll not mind; sure, he's young, plenty of energy. He doesn't need much sleep. I tell you, I didn't need much sleep when I was playing out round the country at his age.'

'Aye, well, so you never stop telling me. Anyway, you can ring him yourself then.'

And there are times when the two of them have to make judgements as well as practical decisions about potential contributors.

'They played with us once before, and they weren't that good.'

'I know, you're right, but they're dead keen to do it again.'

'In fact, they weren't that good at all.'

'Oh, I know, I know, but what can we say? It's very hard to turn people down.'

'Well, I think we'll have to. Sure, you can think of something.'

'No, you do it – it'll sound better coming from you. And anyway, that's why you have the privilege of being my producer.'

His producer is clearly enjoying herself in Irvinestown as Hugo welcomes back his listeners after the two o'clock news. This is a good one. The running order is going to plan and the music guests are on cue; the band is as tight as the proverbial drum and in top form; Hugo is in fine tune, stretched to twanging point like an elastic band; and the crowd, by any conservative estimate, numbers six hundred.

The dance floor is packed close up to the stage; they're standing ten deep at the back and there are so many in the balcony that there's some talk as to whether the structure can take the weight. Hugo suggests that anyone over twelve stone should come back down the stairs, but no one takes any heed.

So it's the opportune moment to serve afternoon tea. Unlike the city, where you only get what you order and get nothing if you don't, no social occasion in the country is complete without tea. The hotel girls fight their way through the crowds with tottering piles of cups and saucers, jugs of milk, industrial-size teapots, bowls of sugar, piles of tray bakes and, in a moment of Joe Mahon supreme inspiration, plates and plates heaped with shamrock-shaped shortbread.

'Look at these!' shouts Hugo as he bites into a piece. 'Saint Paddy's shortbread and you'll all get a bit, for there's one for . . . '

And as he points his microphone at the crowd they dutifully roar back, 'Everyone in the house!'

The crowd is boisterous, jovial, noisy; there is laughter, shouting, clapping; they are every age and every background and they know each move of the show as if they'd written out the running order themselves. These are people whose social interaction is rehearsed over years and they feel easy.

Foster and Allen take the stage and this audience is so familiar with the entertainment that, without any prompt, it accompanies the duo in their long-time hit, some singing heartily while others mouth the words to themselves almost casually as they gaze round the room:

> Old flames can't hold a candle to you
> No one can light up the night like you do
> Flickering embers of love
> I've known one or two
> But old flames can't hold a candle to you.

In the midst of it all, now on the floor amongst the joyful throng, is Hugo. He's eager to find out more about the folk who've turned up today and as soon as he asks, 'Where are you from?' it's clear that the appeal of an afternoon in his company extends far beyond the main street of Irvinestown. The responses come back: Dromore, Ballinamallard, Moygashel, Hamiltonsbawn, Trillick, Banbridge, Armagh, Dundonald, Mallusk.

'Mallusk?'

'Yes, we came down on the bus this morning and we had our lunch here in the hotel and we're having a wonderful time.'

'And are you having a wee drink?'

'I am surely. Why, do you want a sip?'

Others aren't just as quick on the ball.

'Anyone you'd like to say hello to?' Hugo prompts.

'Oh, let me think now.'

'That's OK, I'm not going anywhere for a while. Anybody? Friends, perhaps?'

'Let me see.'

'I can come back in an hour's time. What about the family? Have you got any family yourself?'

'I have, aye.'

'How many?'

'Just the one.'

'I'm not a bit surprised; it probably took you that long to make up your mind and say yes! Good luck to you anyway and we're delighted you're with us this day. Ladies and gentlemen, please give a big Saint Patrick's Day welcome to my friend from Branson in the USA, Mr Moe Bandy!'

The cheers ring up from the dance floor as Moe takes the stage and the band leads him into one of his American hits, 'Bandy the Rodeo Clown'. At the latter end of his career, Moe is still one of those names that an Irish country audience recognises instantly, for his reputation was built on a honky-tonk style of singing that echoes the songs sung here; songs to do with love, drinking, cheating and humour, the storytelling type of song that Hugo has always enjoyed. And what Hugo enjoys just as much is that Moe has come with an invitation for him.

14

'I want you to come over and visit me in Branson,' Moe says. 'All my country friends live there and we would love for you to come and sing with us and do your radio show from my theatre.'

Moe Bandy refers to owning his own theatre the way you might talk about having a modest garden shed.

'Do you hear that, folks?' Hugo shouts with delight. 'You're all witnesses. Moe has invited me to Branson. The only trouble is, Moe, I can't go anywhere unless the bosses allow me, so I'll have to persuade Maggie and Susan back in Belfast to let me go – they're the ones with the money.'

'Are they your bosses? OK, Maggie, Susan, you all got to let my friend Hugo come and visit me in my house. I don't mind when; just bring the band and everything. You hear me now?'

By now, Hugo is on to his fourth tin of Red Bull and those in the crowd at the front of the hall are trying to get to the bar at the back, while those at the bar are trying to get to the front to be closer to the crack. Meanwhile, some people upstairs want to come down, and those who've been pushed out the door into the entrance area are pushing upstairs in the hope of finding some space.

Basically, everyone is on the move to somewhere else in the hall, and on top of this, there's another hundred or so sitting outside in the sunshine, listening to the music coming through the open doors and on car radios.

As three o'clock approaches, the programme winds up to its finale. For the past ninety minutes Hugo has never moved out of sight of his audience. Down on the floor, he's always among them. When he introduces a singer on stage, he stands to the side; he never leaves the spotlight entirely. He keeps his microphone in hand for the moment when he might join in. Not for a second is there any doubt as to whose show this is.

Now, at three minutes to three, Hugo is back on stage leading the applause as he thanks his guests, the band, Davy, Davy and George, Joe Mahon, the hotel staff, listeners at home, the audience in the hall, Saint Patrick, Trish Coyle from the banks of the Foyle and the Wee Woman with the Big Stick, Joanne Murphy. He has been in constant motion since the programme began and now he's bouncing about like a puppet that's got its strings mixed up.

The band shifts into the opening bars of 'Amarillo' that they rehearsed earlier and as Hugo shouts 'Goodbye from Irvinestown' one more time, the crowd sha-la-las along with the song and the music fades away under the pips and the jingle that announces the Radio Ulster news at three o'clock.

It will be another hour before Hugo can leave the hall. There are autographs to sign, photos to be posed for, hands to be shaken yet again, more kisses, more hugs, stories to be told and promises to be made to meet again soon. He won't wind down for hours; it's unlikely he'll go to bed much before two in the morning. He'll be torturing himself about how to take Moe Bandy up on his offer to visit the States. At half nine the next morning, he'll get into the car of the day to drive to Belfast and do the whole thing again.

And it's only Monday.

2

Wee Susie

When it became known that Susanne Duncan was pregnant and there was no talk of marriage, the news must have set a few tongues wagging in Townsend Street in Strabane. There's nothing like a bit of scandal to liven up the local gossip, and the plight of Wee Susie, as she was affectionately known, must have raised an eyebrow or two. But even in 1950, when attitudes to marriage, illegitimate children and a woman's place were much less liberal than they are today, her pregnant and unmarried state does not appear to have caused the stir that one might imagine. She was an accepted and respected member of the community and a devout attender at chapel – the Church of the Immaculate Conception – all her days. Much of her spare time was spent helping to organise church and parish social events and both she and Hugo were welcome in houses up and down Townsend Street.

This didn't stop some folk from reminding Hugo, as a child and as an adult, that they knew where he came from. As a youngster, it rolled over him; in later years, he put it down to some peculiar twist in those who insisted on mentioning it.

Susie had grown up in Townsend Street, continued to live there after Hugo was born, had several close friends who lived nearby, and yet there is no complete story to explain why she did not get married and why she clearly chose to have the baby with every intention of raising the child herself. 'Wee Susie was thirty-nine years old when she gave birth to me,' Hugo says. 'I was her only child. She'd no husband, no man, no family – just me. And she always told me she was happy.'

If she was considering marriage at all, Susie would have been expected to marry quite a few years before this, but, although she had boyfriends, there is no evidence that she ever received a proposal of marriage, or that she set her cap at any man. It's possible that her independent spirit may have set her against marriage. Close to forty, she would have been considered to be on the shelf, an old maid, a spinster, terms that Hugo clearly hates being used to describe his mother's status in the world:

> Some time after she died I got a copy of the death
> certificate and it said on it beside Occupation or Status
> – Spinster. And that made me so angry because
> 'spinster' was always used in the same breath as talking
> about a woman who hadn't done much with her life,
> and as far as Susie was concerned, she had lived a life
> full of incident and love and friends, even though she
> never married.

Hugo's father was Packie McGlynn, and although he may not have lived with them, Susie made sure that from an early age Hugo knew his identity. Sixty years ago, Strabane was a small town and she knew that if she didn't tell Hugo who his father was, it was certain that someone else would. Packie's nickname was Pokey, and the fact that this same nickname was passed on to Hugo when he was at school is testament that his father was known in the area. There was no surprise in this, for Packie McGlynn ran a cobbler's business in the town. He moved out of Strabane shortly after Hugo was born, and although Hugo knew where Packie lived until his death, he met his father only once.

Other than giving him the most basic facts, Susie never engaged in any further conversation with Hugo about his father – what he was like, if she ever saw him again, and certainly nothing about her feelings for him, whether they had considered marriage and why he made no appearance in Hugo's world, ever. As a child, none of these considerations entered Hugo's head for he had no particular interest in his father; Hugo's world was his mother and he had no reason to wonder what having a father might be like, because, quite simply, he never knew one. 'Wee Susie was father and mother to me,' he says. 'I have always said, no offence meant, that I was like a man born without a limb, I was lacking something but I did not and could not know what it felt like ever to have had it. If he'd been around for a few years and then gone away, then, yes, I think my feelings as a child would have been very different.'

For many years, Hugo believed that Susie's pregnancy was accidental but, in latter years, he has wondered if she may perhaps have felt, in the absence of any other family, that this was her chance to create something of her own. Susie had no close family. There was a brother, Hugh, who died when he was young, and her parents were dead. She had some distant relations who wanted her to have Hugo adopted but she steadfastly refused, and from that point on, their interest in her seems to have disappeared. Hugo never knew any of Susie's family, and Joan recalls that from the time of their engagement, leading up to their marriage, when members of the two families would normally have been gradually introduced to each other at various social functions, there was never, ever, a mention of anyone from Susie's side. Susie's lifelong friend and Hugo's godmother, Madeline Duffy, told Hugo late in her life that Susie never talked about her family, though Madeline had known them.

Until a few years ago, Hugo assumed that his father had scarpered, beaten a hasty retreat when he'd discovered that Susie was pregnant, but recently he has learned that there had been talk of marriage, to the extent that Packie and Susie had met with one of the local priests and discussed the matter. Theirs was not a brief relationship, an assumption he'd also made, nor did his father leave because there was a third party involved. However, a wedding never materialised and there is no one now to suggest why that might have been. The story is further complicated at this point, for at some stage Susie visited Packie's shop and they had a falling out over an issue unknown, with the result that she smashed the window in the shop. It was shortly after this incident that Packie moved his business to Castlederg.

These days it is not at all uncommon for a woman to want children without the ties of marriage or even a permanent relationship with the father of her children. In Susie's day such an approach to motherhood would have attracted much more controversy. Imagine her position – unmarried, approaching forty, pregnant, on her own and living in a small town in rural Ireland in 1950. But Hugo knows that criticism wouldn't have deterred her, for one thing that has become very clear to him as he reviews what little he knows of her circumstances at the time of his birth is that she was very set on having him and, once he was born, keeping him. 'Whatever people thought of her,' he says, 'she must have been a bit scared, but she was a very determined woman and she never backed away from anything. She would far sooner see things through to the bitter end rather than avoid them, and I am very like that too.'

Hugo was born on 26 March 1950. He was christened Hugh Anthony, and Hugh is what he was always called by Susie and what she wrote on the back of the early black-and-white photographs of her young son. She had no nickname for him, even though others called him Shugo, Shuey or Hugo. She hated these names and anyone who used them in her company would quickly realise that she had a sharp tongue. Hugo weighed somewhere between three and four pounds when he was born and was so small that his first cot was a shoe box. He must have eaten well, for not long after the box was replaced by a drawer out of the dresser.

Hugo and his mother lived at 27 Townsend Street in an area known as the Head of the Town. The house was a small two-up, two-down terrace; at the rear was a small yard with its outside lavatory and then a slope that ran straight down to the river bank. The front of the house opened directly on to the street. If you drive along Townsend Street today, the terrace has gone and a grass verge and a few council wastepaper bins mark the spot where the Wee Man from Strabane took his first steps and clapped excitedly as the accordion band swung down the road into the town.

The house was rented at a sum of two shillings per week from the Campbells, two spinsters and their two bachelor brothers who lived next door. Like Madeline, the Campbells were good neighbours to Susie and were always kind to Hugo. They had taken Susie under their wing and she found in them some of the comfort and support that she missed in the absence of a close family. They were also a considerable influence on Hugo, for, although in his young eyes they were very old, they were part of the adult group that surrounded him as he grew up. One initial consequence of not having a father, coupled with the fact that his mother had no direct family, was that there was no natural grouping that Hugo could call his own, other than the adults who touched on his mother's life. Once he started to explore the world beyond his small terrace, he began to fall in with others of his own age, but grown-ups were always in the background.

The terrace house was Hugo's home until he was well into adulthood, and no matter the circumstances of his birth, it was a happy home, one in which he felt confident and loved. Among other jobs that she took on, Susie was a home help and her own house was always neat and clean, or at least, one half of it was neat and clean. For the first years of Hugo's life, he and Susie lived on the ground floor only, the upper floor being useful only for storage. Gradually it was made more habitable but it was dark, so, as a confident young teenager, Hugo took it upon himself to install the electricity upstairs. This involved running a length of wire from a light bulb extension from the downstairs hall and, using a series of extensions, simply plugging into it everything that was required on the new floor.

The thought that he was doing anything dangerous didn't enter

Hugo's head. Then years later he related his electrical skills to an electrician friend, who listened in silence. When Hugo had finished his tale, his friend proceeded to tick off a list that included no earth, no fuses and, with the old AC current, a very high chance of getting an electric shock or burning down the whole house and half the street with it. 'And the electric shock wouldn't just have been a buzz, he said it would have killed me' – Hugo smiles wryly – 'there'd be a lot of music lovers very happy with that, eh?'

Susie was always busy and photographs show her wearing her apron as if she's been interrupted for a moment at some task around the house. Housework was done to the accompaniment of the radio, or if she was out of its range, she would create her own music and sing to herself; 'Carolina Moon' and 'Two Little Girls in Blue' were a couple of particular favourites.

> One little girl in blue, lad,
> Won your father's heart.
> She is your mother, I married the other
> But now we have drifted apart.

Hugo's earliest memories echo to the sound of the radio in his home – a big Philips receiver tuned eternally to Radio Éireann:

> There was always music, ceilidh bands, traditional,
> dance music, the crooners. Wee Susie loved it all,
> everything she did was done to the music on the radio
> and she sang along to it. If she didn't know the words,
> she made them up, and if she didn't make them up, she
> just hummed. It's well over fifty years ago, but if I close
> my eyes, I can see and hear her again, singing along to
> the radio.

At the time of his birth, for many, the radio was still an amazing piece of technology, placed in the kitchen or living room where the whole family could listen to it. The radio had presence – that was guaranteed by its size alone – and in most houses it was an item of furniture as well as a companion. The most popular show on Radio Éireann was the *Sunday Night Play*, and to ensure that Susie wouldn't miss the beginning, it was Hugo's job to make certain the radio was turned on a good five minutes before the programme began. As far as he was concerned, there was undoubtedly something mysterious, even magical, about it:

> You'd turn the radio on and nothing would happen for
> a while. At first the music sounded far away until
> suddenly it was in the room with you. I remember, as a
> young cub, thinking that the different bands and
> orchestras all had their own rooms and every time a
> new piece of music came on all that was happening was
> that we were listening to another room.

The old radios heated up, becoming warm to the touch. Hugo and Susie's kitchen was lit by the glow of the radio and the flicker of the stove, and there was a smell of burning dust and Bakelite. There was a tuning knob and a red or green line would pick out the names etched on the Perspex screen – Hilversum, Athlone, Luxembourg . . . Accompanying it all was the crackle that assured the listeners not only that the technology was working but that these voices and sounds were coming from places far beyond their kitchens and hearths. Hugo recalls:

> I find it amazing now that people contact me from
> America, Australia, all over the world, and they're
> sitting there listening to me on their wireless networks
> or on their computers. And yet I'm no more amazed
> than when I was a wee lad reading out those places on

the dial and listening to boys telling me they were broadcasting that evening from Dublin or London. Those were places far beyond Strabane and Wee Susie's house, places you had to look for on a map.

Many years later, radio gave Hugo his second career, but it would be a long time before BBC Radio Ulster appeared on that dial. These were the days of the Northern Ireland Home Service, when the news was presented in accents never heard at Strabane market, and the BBC's only entertainment radio service, the Light Programme, lifted the gloom of the early fifties with *The Billy Cotton Band Show*.

Susie had little money and it is clear that what she did have was spent totally on Hugo, who was never aware of any sense of deprivation. He had a bike, several over the years, his pride and joy. When he decided to become a drummer, the Provident cheque was used to buy him a set of drums. For someone like Susie who had little capital, the Provident cheque was one of the ways to get credit, for she could borrow a sum of money and pay it back in weekly instalments. Only certain shops accepted the Provident cheque, and if Susie needed to buy goods elsewhere, she would enter into other hire purchase arrangements, as she did when she bought Hugo a tape recorder from Cavendish's in Derry, where she had got the radio. Most goods, large and small, were bought on credit in some shape or form and paid for in instalments. This was how people made purchases in those days, how they afforded big items. It was how business was conducted. Even the day-to-day purchases Susie made in her local shops were 'paid in for' in the shopkeeper's book, where a note was kept of what was owed and a deduction made each time some of it was paid off.

Hugo certainly wasn't undernourished. Susie cooked the staple fare – plenty of potatoes, and there was always bacon and cabbage on the go. Sausages and mince formed part of the diet and some of the best stuff was on the doorstep, for the half of Strabane was reared on Doherty's mince, indeed, the half of Derry too. There was Ordinary Mince and Special Mince and Wee Susie was always very specific about what she wanted. She'd give Hugo his instructions before he went off on his errands: 'Remember now, Hugh, tell him it's for me and you want the Special.'

He was no stranger to the bakeries, either, and was a regular visitor at Doran's in Meetinghouse Street and at Russell's. These two establishments helped him develop the taste for cream buns that many years later he would turn into a regular feature on his radio show, inviting his listeners to put the kettle on and have their 'Afternoon Tea with Hugo D'. His sweet tooth was nurtured too by Madeline, who was renowned for her baking, and Hugo visited her house every day to sample her cakes and buns. All his early photographs show a thriving child with a plump face, who appeared to get rounder as he got taller. When he became a young altar boy, one of the nuns foresaw a future career far removed from the one he eventually took. She patted his round stomach under its cassock and observed: 'Sure you have the makings of a good bishop on you, young Hugo.'

The shops were also a social network, where people met, news was gathered and gossip passed on. Customers knew each other and the shopkeepers knew them all and their families too. 'From when you were very wee,' says Hugo, 'you were always sent on messages, and going in and out of the different shops meant people got to know you and would look out for you. So Susie would never have been worried where I was because she knew that someone would always see me.'

One of the reasons that Susie was popular in her street was that she enjoyed helping others and she saw Hugo as a natural extension of her ability to do just that. She sent him on messages for the neighbours, the Campbells next door, the Bannigans across the street, and off he'd head with a note clutched in his hand or a simple order recited over and over again before he was let go. There wasn't much danger of him getting mugged, for there was nothing to take, no money changed hands, every shopkeeper had that same book in which all transactions were noted, and the bills were settled at another time or whenever it could be afforded.

There was a financial advantage to being known by the shopkeepers. As well as receiving the odd treat as he went about his messages, Hugo found future employment in the home delivery service offered by many of the shops. Two of the local shopkeepers, Mrs Baxter and Nellie Traynor, shared the use of a grocer's delivery bike, and from time to time, the ladies employed Hugo's short legs to transport customers' goods. A touch accident prone, he narrowly avoided having his prospects as a future father being wiped out when he was stopped by a wall after the brakes on the bike didn't work. On another occasion, the brakes worked too well and he sailed over the handlebars, cracking a few teeth in the process. Thanks to a bit of nifty dental work, the engaging smile survived. He also delivered papers every Sunday after Mass, collecting them from Packie McDevitt's sweet shop, or to be more accurate, from the half-door that led into the hallway at the side of the shop. He delivered them to the big houses at the edge of town, which, no matter what direction you travelled, entailed cycling uphill.

There were other diversions too. The town was a busy rail connection, with goods being carried to all parts of the country, and it was in relation to this that Hugo got one of his first jobs. Across the road from where he lived was a garden nursery owned by the Bannigans. Because the railway through Strabane went to Derry, Donegal, down the west coast of Ireland, and across to Belfast and beyond, a lot of their plants were transported on the train. 'I remember as a wee lad,' says Hugo, 'I'd be given boxes to take down to the station and they were carried in the guard's van. Everything travelled by train. There were bicycles, parcels, barrels, even animals. On a good day, the trip to the station with a few boxes could last for hours, for there was so much to see down at the yards.'

The bond between Susie and her son was extraordinarily close; it could not have been otherwise. He was the one person she could regard as her family; she was the one who absorbed the stigma they both bore and did everything right by him, as much as it was in her power to do so. Susie was fiercely protective of him; he was her world and her joy. It was typical of her nature that she refused to pretend that life was anything other than what it was, nor would she allow it in others. 'I remember so clearly,' says Hugo, 'the day she and I were shopping in the town and someone started to chat to her. I was just a cub and the lady studied me and said, "Oh, he's very like . . . you know, the spitting image of . . . you know who," and Wee Susie says, "Oh, you can say it straight out, sure he knows all about it." And I was so proud of her for saying that, for standing up for us.'

Susie was a tiny woman, just under five feet, with a small face that lit up readily into a smile. She conducted a constant search for shoes because she took only a size two and they were almost impossible to find. The congregation always knew when she came into the chapel because her tiny feet made a distinctive *clip-clop* on the wood and stone floor. She was a sociable woman who enjoyed a day out, an excursion, and people liked her. An old black-and-white photograph shows Susie and Hugo along with some neighbours, standing outside Boyle's Green Café. Everyone is dressed up, Susie in her two-piece with her bag under her arm, holding her gloves. The ten-year-old Hugo standing beside her with the big ice cream is nearly as tall as his mother.

There were always callers at the house, for Susie was one of those who understood the filling in of forms, the sort of language they required, and could be counted on to come up with a few good reasons which the applicant could use to twist the arm of the Housing Executive to get an extra grant or bit of work done. She was a very practical woman who clearly wasn't squeamish, for one of her jobs in the Head of the Town was as a washer of bodies, a job she shared with Hannah Stewart. They would be called to the house of a dead neighbour to wash and tidy the body for the undertaker, and although it was a job that had to be done, the mere thought of what Wee Susie was doing fairly put the wind up her son:

> She came in one night straight from over the road
> where she had been washing down a neighbour who
> had died, and when I was small, I would sleep in the
> bed with her. In she came, straight from the body and
> got into the bed. I wasn't long getting out of it and I
> didn't get back in. As far as I was concerned, the last
> thing she'd touched was a corpse and the next thing
> she touched wasn't going to be me.

Susie may not have been squeamish and she may have been a good Christian, but she was also extremely superstitious, as was Madeline, and her superstitious nature is something that Hugo has inherited. Here were two women he trusted, who were devout in their attendance at chapel and talked in sincere tones of how they knew that 'certain things were meant to be'. Susie 'knew' when a death was imminent. In Our Lady's Grotto, a shrine built on the site of an old church just across the road from the house, a little bell was rung to mark the services, but if it rang when no one was near it, then it was a certain sign of tragedy.

Hugo knew this to be true, because when he was a child, he had heard the bell and, within a day, a neighbour was dead. He and Susie were visiting their neighbour, Annie, in her small house just as her husband, Jocky, came home from work. He went through to the narrow scullery at the back to change out of his work clothes. Jocky was a big man, so when there was a thump from the back of the house, Annie sighed, 'There you are, he's knocked something over,' she said, at which point Susie and Hugo went back across the street to their own house. Just as Susie was about to open their front door, Annie came rushing out, screaming that Jocky was dead. The thump had been his body hitting the floor.

Hugo still listens for the bell.

Susie had the air of being somewhat mysterious, for she had a reputation as a reader of teacups. Young girls who were courting would come to her to have their tea leaves read in the hope that this middle-aged, unmarried mother could give them some guidance as to which young man they should set their cap at. And people liked her enough to feel comfortable having a bit of fun with her. On one occasion she was sitting with some of her friends in the kitchen at Saint Patrick's Parochial Hall and they were passing the time, with Susie reading the tea leaves. The priest gave his teacup to one of the girls and told her to give it to Susie but not let on whose it was. He stood outside the door as she recounted aloud who the owner of the cup would meet, who would become the great love of his life and the many years of happy and fruitful marriage that lay before him. When he came in to thank her for the reading, those around the table collapsed in laughter as she drew herself up to her full height and roundly reprimanded him for deceiving her so.

Radio, dance halls and cinema were the major forms of entertainment and Hugo became an ardent film-goer. In the year he was born, John Wayne and Maureen O'Hara starred in *Rio Grande*, directed by John Ford, the film that the studio insisted he make in order to finance his next project, *The Quiet Man*, a film that remains one of Hugo's firm favourites. Going to the pictures was not a habit he picked up from his mother, for she never went and always said she could find no entertainment in them. It seems strange that a woman who loved music and attended every social occasion in her local parochial hall should not at least have been attracted to the blockbuster song-and-dance films of the time, but her son's enthusiasm more than made up for her lack of interest. 'The films would be changed in the middle of the week,' Hugo recalls, 'so I'd go on a Monday or Tuesday. The programme would be changed on a Wednesday and Thursday, so I'd go again. And then to make matters even better, there was a picture house in Lifford just across the bridge and I went there too. Oh, I was hell for the pictures.'

He was such a frequent visitor to the cinema that a local busybody informed the parish priest that Susie was allowing Hugo to indulge in a very sinful practice and she should be spoken to before the young boy was damned for ever. The priest knew Susie to be a staunch supporter of the chapel and all its activities, and as he wasn't beyond attending the odd John Wayne epic himself, nothing came of the matter.

Although she never saw anything on the big screen, Susie became enthralled by the small screen during the fifties, as television grew in popularity. When the first television set arrived in Townsend Street, she wasn't long in tracking it down. The set belonged to Hughie and Kathleen Malugh, who lived just across the street, and it arrived when Hugo was about seven or eight years old. Programmes were broadcast for only a few hours every day and Susie would call at Hughie and Kathleen's door on some errand or other, just as the programmes were starting. It soon became routine for her and Hugo to have their tea and then spend the next couple of hours with their neighbours, who rarely managed to enjoy their latest luxury in peace.

Susie was not always in the best of health and Hugo recalls that when he was very young the doctor would give her injections, after which she would have to take to her bed, simply closing up the house, unable to do any work. Hugo would go to bed with her till the pain had passed. It's not clear what her problem was, although he has always assumed that it was to do with gallstones, but it was severe enough to warrant short hospital stays. On these occasions, Susie's good turns in the community were reciprocated, and Hugo would stay with Gerry and Maggie McAuley, neighbours who lived in the wonderfully named Puddle Alley.

Hugo went to Barrack Street Primary School just down the road from his home and he remains proud of the prize he was awarded for not missing a day at school. As well as showing that he was in excellent health, it's also an indication of how keen his mother was to make sure that he had the best opportunity and that he should realise the importance of being reliable and punctual. These are qualities Hugo has tried to carry with him though his life. And today, once he commits himself to a gig, charity appearance, photo call, once he makes a promise to a listener or fan to visit or give them a mention, he stands by his word. He doesn't let others down and that was a lesson instilled by Susie.

Hugo enjoyed primary school. He doesn't recall applying himself that hard to the work, but then, neither did he find it a chore. If there were remarks made about his lack of a father, they didn't make any impact on him, although he was confused when people addressed him by his father's nickname, Pokey; confused, not because it hurt, but simply because it wasn't his name. Aside from those attempting to make mischief, he had no problem finding friends in Townsend Street to run about with and it was the same at school. He felt no different from the others, except that he couldn't quite get the hang of the large extended families from which his fellow pupils came. It wasn't so much that he wanted one, he just wasn't used to grannies, grandpas, aunts and uncles.

Barrack Street Primary School is still open and stands beside the chapel and across the road from Saint Pat's Hall, and it's within this small triangle that Hugo began to get a taste of the experience that would ultimately set him on the road in the music business, for what Hugo enjoyed most was performance. Like all small children, he acted out little stories in class, he sang in Sunday school, he was dressed up and had his hair smoothed down so that he looked angelic, and he realised that it was good fun and he enjoyed it. 'I could sing,' says Hugo. 'I had a good sense of timing and rhythm. The more I did it, the more I realised that I liked it. I enjoyed getting the compliments and people patting me on the head and telling me I was a great wee man.'

And the wee man had plenty of opportunity to seek out the compliments, because, from an early age, he was included in any choir, play or pantomime that was going. This was due in part to his talent and in part to the fact that Saint Pat's Hall became almost a second home to him. Much of Susie's social life and a number of her odd jobs were centred on the hall, which was a popular venue for activities and clubs. She ran the cloakroom and served teas, as well as helping with the various functions that took place there. Many of these involved entertainment and music and Hugo's earliest memories of the hall include people performing on a stage or on some designated area on the floor. Songs, recitations, stories – everyone had a party piece and Hugo learned quickly that he could wheedle his way into any entertainment because he was Wee Susie's child and he was like part of the furniture.

'Precocious' is one of the terms that might be used to describe him in his early years, with a tendency to get in the way, but he's also remembered as an engaging young performer who had a tuneful and decent voice and it wasn't long till he gave his first solo singing performance in the hall, with a rendition of 'Around the World I've Searched for You'. 'I was there every guest tea, every concert at Saint Pat's, not so much entertaining people as torturing them,' Hugo laughs.

If he tortured them, he also charmed them, and it was in Saint Pat's that he first realised that one of the ways to keep an audience looking in his direction was to give them what they wanted.

The chapel and all its activities occupied a great deal of Susie's time. She was one of those who attended everything and was very particular about observing all the rituals and saints' days; thus a large part of Hugo's time was also spent on ecclesiastical matters. Just as with the neighbours and local shopkeepers, he appears to have been 'volunteered' out. As an altar boy, he was good at the job, and clearly the priests thought so too, for despite his complaints that early morning services in winter weren't much fun, Hugo performed the role for many years. One of his tasks was to hold the large missal, from which the priests read the responses. On one occasion this led to a bit of unintended entertainment:

> It's a big chapel and there are three different levels around the altar, so I would parade around carrying the book, which was quite heavy. One Sunday I was genuflecting in front of the altar and I was a wee bit too close to the edge of the top step. I could feel my heels slipping backwards and then the whole lot went, me, the robes, the big book, my legs, all up in the air. It's amazing how much noise one wee boy can make in a big chapel.

He may have been an altar boy but he wasn't always good. Above all, his pride and joy was his bike and he was the scourge of the neighbourhood. Hugo travelled everywhere on the bike, usually on the pavement or the wrong side of the road, and paid no heed to Halt or Give Way signs. His status as altar boy and part-time bell ringer didn't do much for him when he almost damaged Father Gillespie's pride and joy, his big Austin Cambridge car. Perhaps the priest was more taken with it than a man in his position should have allowed, but that was between him and God, so woe betide anything or anybody that damaged it:

> I was flying down the hill on the bike, and you have to remember, with always being a wee, fat boy, once I got started it was hard to stop, and I shot off the pavement just as Father Gillespie was coming round the corner in the car. He hit the brakes and swerved. He just missed a post and I just missed him. He got me later at the hall and I can remember him standing there, flicking my ear

between every word when he gave off to me: 'You – *flick* – nearly – *flick* – ran – *flick* – into – *flick* – my – *flick* – car – *flick* – Mas – *flick* – ter – *flick* – Dun – *flick* – can.' I can laugh now but it wasn't funny at the time. It was a brave lesson in the Highway Code all the same – *flick*.

His bicycle was also the means by which Hugo engaged in his first bit of smuggling. Lifford, in the Republic of Ireland, and Strabane are separated by nothing more than the river and a bridge, and when no less a person than Madeline, his revered godmother and a dedicated smoker, decided the tax on cigarettes had got too high, she recruited Hugo to do the Sweet Afton Run. Named after a famous cigarette brand, the run entailed taking orders and money from neighbours, cycling across the border, buying cheap cigarettes and cycling back past the customs men, the packets stuffed inside his shirt, with a loose jerkin or pullover on top to conceal the goods.

One Sunday, as he came back through the border, he heard the shout he'd always dreaded.

'Hi, boy!'

There was no one else about, so he knew it was definitely directed at him.

'Hi, boy, hold on there!'

With the shouts ringing after him, he pedalled like he'd never pedalled before. 'It was a hot day,' says Hugo. 'Can you imagine me, eleven stone, wee fat legs flying round, sweat pouring off me, cigarette packets sticking to me and waiting to hear the siren on the car come behind me at any moment!'

Strabane was then still small enough for people to know one another, and a few days later one of the customs officers stopped the young smuggler in the street and put the fear of God into him about what would happen if he was ever caught.

As he walked away, the officer said, 'By the by, young Hugo, next time you try it, don't take such a large order. You looked like the

Michelin tyre man waddling across the bridge.'

Looking back at the boy who was always torturing others – causing accidents on his bike, socialising with neighbours and shop-owners, and gradually learning his trade in the local hall – is to see the man he has become: lively, rarely sitting still, fun-loving and engaged in endless banter. And he's always been inclined to think quite well of himself:

> When I was twelve, I played the part of Buttons in the pantomime, *Cinderella*, in Saint Pat's Hall. I had my own song:
>
> > 'Today I passed you in the street
> > And my heart fell at your feet.'
>
> I loved singing it and the applause I got – it went on and on, and I had to sing the whole song again. I thought I was just the greatest thing, and then when it happened the next night, I turned round and there were the Duffy brothers standing behind me. They were the Ugly Sisters and they were mouthing 'more, more' to the audience and getting everyone to cheer, and there was me thinking I was brilliant.

Mind you, he was brilliant, and he got his picture and his first review in the local paper on 12 January 1963. His mother kept a copy in her box of photographs and clippings, which Hugo found after she died. He still has it: 'Master Hugo Duncan (above) was entertaining in the part of Buttons in the recent production of *Cinderella*.' It hardly set the world alight, but it was a start. And anyway, Wee Susie's pride was clear for all to see and that's all that mattered to Hugo.

He wonders now if his father ever saw him in any of those shows, whether he was even aware of them. When he was a well-known musician in the Strabane area, the notion did come into his head:

I was playing at the Border Inn in Castlederg and for the first time I wondered if my father could have been in the room. It was close to home for him and there would have been posters round the place. He could have been standing in that room and I wouldn't have known. He could have listened, had a drink and slipped away.

But such thoughts came on reflection; they didn't bother him when he was a youngster on the stage in Saint Pat's, for in that environment he felt confident and secure, with no need of a father. Saint Patrick's Hall was, after all, his mother's world, and as long as Wee Susie was there and Hugo had her joyful smile, then the rest of the world couldn't trouble him.

3

The Three-Chord Trick

Even now I find it hard to believe that between the
time of playing Buttons in the pantomime in Saint Pat's
and leaving Saint Colman's Secondary School three
years later, I had learned enough to be getting paid for
playing music for people at weekends.

In his own words, Hugo had been entertaining and torturing
audiences in Saint Pat's and Barrack Street Primary School since he
was able to stand on his own two feet and recite 'My Donegal
Home'. He was in everything; it seemed it wasn't possible to attend
an entertainment evening without young Duncan having some role
in it. Like many other youngsters, he also did the circuit of music
competitions and *feises*, as both solo and ensemble performer.

Feises are competitive festivals of music, verse and dance, held
all over the country in venues large and small, humble and grand.
In Strabane, the *feis* would start on a Friday and carry right on
through the weekend; in Derry it could last a week and more. It
was broken down into categories or classes, with the children's
classes being held usually during the day, but Hugo also loved going
at night, when matters became really serious. That was when the
grown-ups strutted, when choirs who had been arch rivals for
decades would once again lock in competition.

It was at these evening sessions, where familiar airs and lyrics
were trotted out year after year, that Hugo first came across the
songs of Percy French, some of which would eventually form part of
Hugo's set list. 'Are Ye Right There, Michael?', 'Phil the Fluter's
Ball' and 'The Mountains of Mourne' were big favourites, but one

in particular always sweeps him back to his childhood immediately. He only has to hear or sing the opening lines of 'Come Back Paddy Reilly to Ballyjamesduff' to imagine that he's sitting once again in Saint Pat's Hall, aged seven or eight, listening attentively and watching the faces of the adults around him as the words of the familiar song carry round the room.

In those days, the business of child performance was densely populated and highly competitive. There were performance categories for every type of expressive discipline imaginable. It was a serious business. Rivalry was rife and if local adjudicators were thought to give their marks too readily to the pupils of one favoured teacher or another, then others were brought in from Belfast or Dublin. And in a world of one-upmanship, if a music festival wanted to be regarded as a cut above the rest, it might even be tempted to bring its adjudicators in from 'across the water'.

Individual children were entered by their music tutors and elocution teachers; choirs and chorale-speaking groups were entered by church organisations; but the bulk of children's groups were entered by the schools. If there was no star pupil to enter in the local *feis*, that wasn't a problem: the entire class could take part in the ensemble verse-speaking competition (Boys and Girls, Age 9–11). Those who spoke with lisps, or rare country accents, or who couldn't remember anything after the first verse would be placed in the back row. Whether good, bad or indifferent, everyone learned and competed together. 'You were entered by the school, usually as part of a group,' Hugo recalls. 'We were taught to sing together, recite verse together, dance together, play whistles together. And if you couldn't do it properly, you mimed. At that age, in primary school certainly, every word, every note, every beat was the same.' He never felt under any pressure to take part. He loved it, and Susie never pushed him to enter the competitions, though she was expected, like all mothers, to make sure that her child appeared in the correct costume.

In order to deck their child in the best Irish-dancing outfit they could afford, families with little enough money would turn to the paid-in-for book. On the occasion that Hugo's primary school was entered for the big *feis* in Derry, Susie had to add another item to her own book:

> I remember I had a blue cummerbund and matching
> bow tie, but they weren't supplied by the school. They
> were something else that had to be bought, or usually
> made out of bought material. And it all went down in
> the book. Mind you, I thought I was just the thing
> when I was dressed up. Can see myself now – James
> Bond, 007, at the age of ten.

And that was simply the way it happened. At the time Hugo attended *feises*, half the local community knew someone who was competing and they'd all turn out in support. So there were plenty of young Hugos singing, whistling and dancing their way round the country, but as he's very quick to remind those within earshot, he was winning medals; most of the others weren't. He's particularly proud of the day at the *feis* in Derry's Guild Hall when he beat the local town favourite into second place in the Solo Singing for Boys, Aged Eleven class. It instilled a prejudice that he's happy to share to this day: 'Derry people are always told they're great singers. They can sing in Strabane every bit as well. There's me and Paul Brady for a start.'

And already, small coincidences were happening that in later years would be interpreted as signs of the direction in which the music would take him. Several parents drove the boys to Derry and Hugo went with his friend David Coyle, whose father drove a big Ford Zephyr. Within a matter of years, Hugo would be singing alongside David senior in the Melody Aces showband and David liked to boast that he'd spotted the young man's talent at an early age.

Winning was all. There was none of this nonsense that taking part means everything. Stumbling, faltering, at times breaking down in tears on stage in front of an audience rooting for its firm favourites, was considered character-building. In Hugo's case, he learned from those first appearances on the big stage that nerves are part and parcel of the business of entertaining and those who can overcome them and channel them into the performance are the ones who will get most out of the occasion. He was certainly nervous; his main worry was that, because he felt he constantly needed to go to the toilet, he would wet himself on stage. Happily the trousers stayed dry, and when he describes the feeling of going on stage, he uses a rather strange comparison: 'As soon as I hit the boards, I was like Wonder Woman. She spins around and becomes a totally different person. That's me. Even today before an outside broadcast or a TV show, I'm dancing around like a youngster who can't find the yard.'

As part of a school team, he also won a medal for set dancing, dressed this time in a kilt that had been let out an inch or two to accommodate the portly Duncan waistline. He wasn't a dainty dancer, something on which the adjudicator made comment as he presented his summation of the group's performance; when he handed out the medals, he made special mention of 'that young girl who showed great determination in guiding this wee man in the front row round the stage'.

But for all those who achieved little at the *feises*, there were also plenty like Hugo who practised, overcame their nerves, succeeded, and tasted that first buzz that comes from applause, recognition and praise. It's certainly true that the hundreds of showbands crisscrossing Ireland never had any problem finding their brass sections. For years at the festivals, trumpet and cornet players who learned their trade in the Boys' Brigade, the local band or school orchestra had been tooting their way through renditions of 'Oh Mein Papa' in the nervous hope that one of them might be the next

Eddie Calvert, the Man with the Golden Trumpet.

Another great and exciting attraction of Hugo's youth was carnivals. Every town and village, and a few places that could pass only as crossroads, had one big event every year that combined sports, displays, stalls, dances, concerts, picnics, fancy dress, pet and bonny baby competitions – sometimes indistinguishable – talent shows, horse-drawn carts, steam engines, prize sheep and marching bands. Strabane Carnival drew people from all over the North-West. Being the main town between Derry and Enniskillen on a north–south axis and between Letterkenny and Omagh going west to east, Strabane was well positioned. It was regarded as a great shopping town: Linton's and Robinson's for furniture, and if you couldn't find a sofa there, you tried Shields's, which is still there to this day. There was Danny McLoughlin's clothes shop, which Hugo was never out of, and Joe Harley's just in case he wanted a change. It was attractions like these that contributed to the town's commercial reputation, and because it was a major rail junction, shoppers could come by train from all parts.

Its carnival was big enough in the sixties to feature on early local television news bulletins, and archive amateur film footage shows huge crowds gathered in fields around the town, with a seemingly endless parade of bands, organisations and children doing the rounds in bright, sunny weather. But then, most events filmed by amateur enthusiasts at the time had bright, sunny weather, mainly because the film quality of anything shot in dull, wet weather was appalling.

It was at the insistence of one of the carnival organisers, Father McHugh, that Hugo took part in one of his few sporting contests:

> Father McHugh had arranged for a series of boxing
> matches and young Brian McGarrigle and I were put
> into the boxing ring to fight. We must have been about
> eleven. I was billed as Killer Duncan, for if I'd sat on

Brian, I'd have squeezed the life out of him, and though the nickname stuck for many years, for the life of me I can't remember who won.

Carnivals could go on for days and very often through the night as well. Hugo was captivated by them. Captivated at all stages of his childhood through to his teens, for, as he grew older, he could discover fresh attractions each year.

And as each event passed, he realised that much of the excitement and enthusiasm was created by those who provided the music, and for young fans, nothing was more exciting than the marching bands. This was where Hugo got his first taste, not just of giving a performance, but of being a part of something that created its own sound and volume, its own style and presentation, that people could watch and admire as well as listen to, for it was a bit of a show:

> I don't care if you talk about the Twelfth of July, a military parade, a precise brass band or one of those bands where everybody plays as loud as possible and the big drummer wallops the daylights out of the skins, everybody loves a marching band. And the more enthusiasm, the more flair, the higher the stick is thrown, then the greater the enjoyment for the spectators. It's pure entertainment and I loved it. Still do.

The Head of the Town had three accordion bands of its own, led by Arthur Friel, Tom P. Mullan and Sammy Rankin. Hugo joined Arthur's band as a triangle player at the age of ten, which, for a child who had ambitions as a drummer, was quite a quiet start. He had already begun his career as a percussionist in the kitchen with saucepans and wooden spoons, and for a few years he continued practising on anything that came to hand until Susie again took advantage of the Provident cheque and bought him a set of drums.

But banging the drums in the kitchen on your own isn't the same as being waved at and cheered on as you march down the road, jingling and jangling on the triangle, dressed in a fancy uniform. 'We wore black trousers, white shirts and peaked caps that looked a bit like a policeman's hat,' says Hugo. 'I thought there was nothing like it. And I thought there was nothing like me and that I hadn't looked so good since I wore the blue cummerbund at the Derry *feis*.'

Hugo was an eager recruit and was delighted when he progressed from triangle to accordion. Maybe his triangle-playing wasn't as good as he imagined, because he clearly wasn't moved on account of his skills as an accordion player; he only ever knew one tune:

> I was small, so they were able to put me in the middle
> of the row. I had the wit to watch when the other
> players opened their accordions out and in and I did
> the same, so there was plenty of squeezing and not a lot
> of playing. Years later there was a big dispute on *Top of
> the Pops* about whether bands should mime to backing
> tracks or not. I was years ahead of them. Listen to your
> Uncle Hugo, boys, and learn.

Every time he embraced a new activity, and particularly with Arthur's band, he was reinforcing the notion that enjoyment of playing music comes in many forms. Being a small, talented boy on the stage of Saint Pat's was one form; another was being part of an event or spectacle that can persuade people to stand by the road and tap their feet to the music.

The marching bands were hugely popular; they brought people together. They would lead the march to the carnival or festival, with folk falling in behind, and then the bands would lead them back home again, just like the Pied Piper. And it didn't matter what organisations the bands belonged to. A decent marching band remained a decent marching band, and the brass bands of Saint

Eugene's and Saint Joseph's were as much an attraction as the three accordion bands.

These experiences, as both spectator and player, sowed the seed in Hugo's imagination that he could be one of those who created the excitement, one of those who could get people into the dance halls and up on their feet. But for the moment, seeing the pride on the faces of the neighbours was enough; someone might even press a tanner or a bob into his fist. And of course, Wee Susie glowed, for she had her very special moment when Hugo was on band duty. Wherever Arthur's band was marching in the town, whether it was for practice or for real, it would end up back in Townsend Street at Our Lady's Grotto, where the faithful would still say their rosary in the evening. 'We would stop at the Grotto,' Hugo recalls, 'and our last number was always "I Sing a Hymn to Mary", and then Arthur would dismiss us and off we would go. Susie always had tears in her eyes when we played that. I suppose it was a wee bit because it was me playing and a wee bit because she had a lot of faith in Our Lady.'

As well as its carnivals and bands, Strabane was also renowned for other musical entertainment. Saturday nights at the Palidrome in Station Road were regarded as one of the biggest attractions throughout the North-West and the hall played host to the top dance bands in Ireland. Hugo's musical education took place at a time when popular music was evolving rapidly, and the increasing availability of records meant that tastes were changing. In Ireland, with its strong links to folk and traditional music, this led to the evolvement of a music entertainment unique to the island, in which familiar local material was intertwined with the increasingly familiar commercial material. And this music was delivered to its many fans by the showbands. It was through the music of the showbands and their continuing evolution that Hugo got a taste for what would become his interest, his passion, his livelihood and his whole life.

And as far as showbands were concerned, Strabane would boast one of the best – arguably, the one that led the music revolution in

Ireland – the Clipper Carlton. What's more, the band just happened to be based round the corner from Wee Susie's house, though at that time they were known as the Carltons and had only recently changed their name from the Hugh Toorish Band.

There would be many influences on Hugo's musical development but it was indeed significant that he was born into an environment where music was a feature of his daily life and that he lived in a part of town renowned for its musicians, where those who made the music were just as liable to wander down the street as the man who was exercising his greyhounds in readiness for the next meet at Lifford dog track.

The dance halls and dance bands were not the sole attraction. In the early sixties, parochial halls like Saint Pat's were centres of social life every bit as much as the dance halls. Indeed, Saint Pat's was known across the same wide geographical area for the variety and quality of its entertainment. There were music nights, plays, pantomimes, dances, and the very famous 'Doctor Sullivan's Revue'. Doctor Sullivan was a GP, a great man, and he organised, wrote and produced these revue shows, which had a bit of everything in them – singing, sketches, monologues, little plays. They were hugely popular and visitors would come from miles away to Saint Pat's, so that they could say they'd been to the doctor's night. Of course, if Hugo wasn't in the audience for a Doctor Sullivan performance, it was only because he had somehow or another wheedled his way into taking part.

When he was twelve, Hugo left Barrack Street Primary School to attend Saint Colman's. He didn't sit the eleven-plus examination; only certain pupils were selected to take part, the thinking being, possibly, that there was little point in going through the rigmarole of setting the papers and marking them if there was a consensus that the candidate did not stand much chance of success. It didn't worry Hugo, but Susie seemed to take it as a slight, and she took herself up one night to the parish priest's house to demand why her

Hugo wasn't good enough to be put down for the exam. It didn't alter anything, so his future remained as determined, and Saint Colman's it was.

Going to 'the big school' was a shock to the boy who had done more or less as he pleased for the previous eleven years:

> Before you went to Saint Colman's, you had to do a test
> to see what class they'd put you in. I was used to the
> kind teachers at Barrack Street, where everything you
> did was great, and I walked into this classroom at Saint
> Colman's and there was a teacher called Master
> Armstrong. He was a cross man, I tell you. I gave him a
> smile, thinking I'd work the charm, and he lit on me.
> God, I thought, I am in a prison camp.

Fearing the worst, he soon discovered that the new school would follow a similar pattern to that of his primary school days. He was a regular attender who did enough to avoid getting into trouble and he quickly realised that, just like Barrack Street and Saint Pat's, Saint Colman's was interested in pupils who were keen on music, and because of its more diverse range of output, he had an opportunity to explore and extend his musical education.

By now some of the stations available on the big Philips radio were playing a different sort of music. As the fifties moved into the sixties, ballads, with their orchestral backings, were vying for popularity with a more vibrant music from names such as Guy Mitchell, Lonnie Donegan, Tommy Steele, Elvis Presley and Buddy Holly. At the time that Hugo was just about to extend his musical experience in Saint Colman's, an entirely new breed, including the Beatles, the Searchers, the Kinks, and the Rolling Stones, was beginning to dominate the British popular music industry.

All this was happening in a few short years and, already, the showbands, versatile entertainers that they were, had twigged on to the fact that if you could put all these influences and experiences into the dance set, you could come close to pleasing most of the people most of the time. The regular crowd in the Palidrome would have found nothing unusual in a set that included arrangements of a traditional song like 'The Hills of Donegal', a hymn such as 'The Old Rugged Cross', a show song like 'Stranger in Paradise' from *Kismet*, and any one from a long string of Elvis songs that topped the British charts before the Beatles had their first Number One – 'Good Luck Charm', 'Return to Sender', 'Surrender', 'Are You Lonesome Tonight?'. Even today, such a set list would not be regarded as unusual in the country dance hall.

Such a selection of tunes reflected how musical tastes in Ireland differed from those in Britain. The British Top Twenty might be listened to, but many Irish people remained close to the tradition of music in their own communities, if not traditional music as such. And this forms part of the explanation as to why the culture and music that Hugo represents in the twenty-first century continues to sit so easily with hundreds of thousands of people across Ireland. The relationship of Irish listeners to music continues to be happily eclectic.

A glance at the bestselling records of 1964, when Hugo was branching out into his first groups and paid performances, clearly bears this out. Record sales in the United Kingdom were dominated in that year by the Beatles, the Rolling Stones, the Animals, the Kinks, Manfred Mann, the Searchers, Roy Orbison and the Dave Clark Five. In Irish record sales there was something of a tug-of-war going on with these new groups and ballad-based solo singers, the latter clearly the winners. A record that only reached Number Three in Britain spent almost two months at Number One in Ireland – Gentleman Jim Reeves with 'I Won't Forget You'. And throughout that year, the domination of the ballad in the Irish charts was repeated by Dickie Rock singing 'There's Always Me', Eileen Reid with 'Fallen Star' and Butch Moore with 'Down Came the Rain', all of which reached Number One.

It was these high-profile Irish singers that Hugo was listening to, because they were the singers people on the island talked about, theirs were the faces readers searched for in the local papers, and their names on a poster guaranteed full takings at a dance. But like anyone who was fortunate enough to be young as the pop music industry developed in the sixties, he was collecting a music experience that embraced many traditions, tastes and styles – the hymns he sang in chapel, his mother's favourite songs, the party pieces and come-all-ye's at the entertainments in Saint Pat's, his drums, the accordion tunes, the ceilidh dance numbers, traditional Irish ballads, the showbands, and this new music aimed directly at his generation.

This whirlpool of changing tastes and trends brought with it something that also made playing the music a great deal easier. It was no longer necessary to have a large backing band; it wasn't essential to have at least ten or twelve musicians before a band could play the dance halls. Even a small-sized ceilidh group needed a piano, which wasn't the most portable instrument to stick in the back of the van. Music now was being made by young men who simply lifted guitars and played them.

At Saint Colman's, Hugo met Pat Doherty, a teacher who was to prove to be a source of further support for the young musician. Pat recognised the versatile talents of his pupil, and as well as ensuring that Hugo participated in the school's various music groups, he encouraged him to continue to take roles in musicals and pantomimes. Such was Pat's influence that some thirty years after leaving the school, Hugo was still playing with musicians who had been encouraged and inspired by the same teacher.

Thus it was at Saint Colman's that he gave his first performance in a group composed entirely of his peers rather than older musicians. Indeed he was a member of a number of different groups, including the school ceilidh band, which had taken him on as drummer; the dented saucepans and dishes proved their worth in the end. And it was an experience with one of these groups that he quotes to demonstrate that what was considered popular entertainment in one part of the world wasn't regarded as such in other parts:

> Pat got us an audition for RTÉ radio at their Sligo studio and Johnny Guthrie drove us down in Father Mullan's Volkswagen Beetle. I had learned the song 'Island of Dreams', by the Springfields, who were very big at the time, and that's what we did for RTÉ. But they didn't want it. They wanted something that fitted with them, something Irish. When we got back to school and Pat found out about it, he muttered something about the Lord preserving him from the fools and idiots he had to teach and said, 'Why didn't you speak up, Duncan, and sing "Come, Come Beautiful Eileen" for them? That would have done the trick.' That was another of those small lessons that stuck in my head. What's the point in me going off and doing my own thing if that's not what people want?

But probably of most importance during Hugo's time at Saint Colman's was that he learned how to play three chords on the guitar. It's possible his entire musical career would not have developed if it hadn't been for hire purchase and the Provident, for Susie organised yet another cheque. With this, Hugo bought a guitar and a capo, a small metal bar that slips over the neck of the guitar to change the key, and with his three chords, he was able for the first time to call himself a self-sufficient, solo entertainer. Combined with his playing in a number of groups, he continued work as a solo performer for the next five years.

The three-chord trick was very good to him, as it has been for thousands of fumbling guitarists who either find the learning to be difficult or simply want to get on with playing the songs. Once Hugo could play three chords, he immediately had at his fingertips a considerable repertoire of songs, and with the capo, he was able to play in any key he wanted, using those same three chord shapes. This was a perfect arrangement for a fellow who wanted to play the extraordinary mixture of styles and songs that the punters in a local pub would expect to hear. Keeping it simple and straightforward was the trick and it's a philosophy that he has stuck to all his life, both as a musician and a broadcaster.

It is a motto he's happy to share with anyone. Some time in the late eighties he was taken to a recording session in Kildare by producer Tony Loughman. Tony would book good session players and then take along some of his singers to record with them. As well as Hugo, on this occasion another of Tony's stable, Frankie McBride, recorded some tracks and Hugo and Frankie drove down together. Two of the session musicians, Tom Pick and Bobby Dyson, had been flown in from Nashville. They had both played with Elvis and Jim Reeves, so they knew their stuff. The songs to be recorded at that session were of the sort to be found on any Hugo Duncan album, and the deal was that Hugo would pick the tracks he wanted to record and Tom and Bobby would arrange them. A bit too elaborately for his taste, as it turned out:

> They were playing all these fancy chords, nearly a different one for each note of the tune, and I said to them: 'No harm to you boys but you should keep it Black Pudding.' They quizzed the engineer about this strange expression and he says, 'Oh Hugo means, keep it simple,' and they laughed, for they knew rightly they were messing about with a simple tune. So that's what I did with the three chords, kept it Black Pudding.

His mother bought him a small, reel-to-reel tape recorder,

purchased as usual on HP from Cavendish's in Derry, and Hugo was now recording tape after tape of ballads, crooners, skiffle, rock-and-roll and pop songs off the radio, engineering them all to fit his three chords. Aged fourteen or fifteen, he was playing in groups and sitting in with a couple of ceilidh bands now and again, but what was taking more and more of his time and interest was playing on his own, starting out at weekends in pubs round the town. He was playing the songs he heard from Ireland's top showband leaders – Dickie Rock, Joe Dolan and Brian Coll – but he could turn his hand to pop tunes as well. 'See me, see the Beatles – no problem,' says Hugo. 'I've done this all my life. Even a song like Frank Sinatra's "My Way" – which has seventh chords, diminished, augmented, cemented or whatever chords – can be played on just three.' His theory of music is that if he hangs on to the chord for long enough, it'll come round again eventually and before he knows it, he's back on track.

He wasn't earning big money, but it wasn't just for beer and tips, maybe two to three pounds a night at a time when a pound had serious purchasing power, and Hugo was playing two or three gigs every weekend. Some further investment in the equipment and he progressed to being something of a one-man band when he bought a microphone and a WEM Echo amplifier. Now he was employed as the turn at weddings and parties and could get a fiver, no problem. Not old enough to drive, the deal would include a lift to and from the function. He was getting used to the high life.

When he wasn't playing music, he worked in his cousin Scobie's pub. On Saturday nights he would take home a bottle of Monk Export and a miniature of Tullamore Dew whiskey for Susie. He had money in his pocket. 'It's funny the wee things you do that become a habit,' he recalls. 'From the time I began to bring in a few pounds, every night I would put some of the money under my mother's pillow and kiss her goodnight. I did that up until the day I was married.'

But if playing at weekends and his increasing work with other groups and bands brought in welcome pounds, shillings and pence, it set a pattern at a very young age that would dominate his life from then until now; playing music consumed his social life:

> It's clear as day to me now. When I was very small, I
> lived with my mother and adults. As I got older I hung
> around Saint Pat's and was involved in everything
> going, and then when I was a teenager, when other
> ones were meeting and going out together, I was away
> playing music. So I did very little of the normal
> socialising that a youngster would do, the way my
> daughter, Suzanne, did when she was growing up, or
> the way the grandchildren do now.

Playing music introduced Hugo to a routine that simply meant when most other people were enjoying themselves, he had to work, and if he wanted to be the one who helped them enjoy themselves, this came with the job:

> I told Joan that I wasn't going to accept any bookings
> for New Year's Eve, 2007, and we suddenly realised that
> it would be the first time in nearly forty years that I
> wouldn't be out playing, and the two of us could hardly
> believe it, but that's true. In this business, from the first
> days to the last, your time is always everybody else's.

This entertainer's routine had a further consequence when Hugo turned professional, because he then realised that when most other people are at their work, he would have time on his hands, sometimes too much time.

4

A Wedding and a Funeral

Hugo left Saint Colman's and after a brief spell at the tech, in 1966 he went to work at the Adria Nylon Factory. The biggest employer in the town, its workforce was drawn from neighbouring villages as well as from Strabane itself. This was boom time and the factory was operating twenty-four hours a day. With such a large number of shift workers, it was a huge social pool as well as a place of work. Economically it was of enormous importance to the area, so not only was it a major employer, it was well respected, and if a young man could gain a place, he was reckoned to be fairly secure, with the prospect of a long-term future in the factory. Hugo's mother therefore regarded the job as a very satisfactory outcome for one who'd never done his eleven-plus, and she was happy that her son was settled, bringing in a decent wage. For, just turned sixteen, Hugo's pay packet was £1.19s.0d. and his first job was to 'wheel a trolley carrying stuff' from one part of the factory to another.

Apart from the money and his mother's blessing, there were several other aspects to the job that appealed to a young fellow just left school. It left his evenings and weekends free for music, and there were plenty of girls to look at. In common with most textile factories, Adria relied on women to make up the bulk of its workforce, with females outnumbering their male colleagues by fifteen to one, so the chances were that one or two might catch his eye. A green young boy like him was also the object of much teasing from the older women, who were happy if they could bring a blush to his cheeks, and his education, one could say, was expanded as he listened to them.

Here he was, in his first job, surrounded by women of all ages. He had started to take an interest in girls when he was still at school, but the talent in the nylon factory must have made a considerable impression on him because he took a rather drastic step; he went on a diet.

All the photographs of Hugo in his early teens reveal a shape that listeners and concert-goers would be familiar with today. He favoured ribbed sweaters and button-up cardigans to accommodate his waistline, and his face, always cheery, had a plumpness to it that gave him a vaguely cherubic air. This was a look that might have suited Buttons in the pantomime or endeared him to the older neighbours as he squeezed his one tune out of the accordion beside Our Lady's Grotto, but it certainly wasn't going to raise the pulses of the factory girls or progress his courting skills. So even though he had a growing reputation as something of an entertainer, a boy who could sing a song or two, he decided that it was time to do something about his image.

When he started in the factory, he weighed close on sixteen stone. This resulted from a combination of Susie's spuds and bacon, his regular visits to the local sweet shops, and fifteen years of eating as many of Madeline's buns and cakes as she could bake. His waistline benefited also from his habit, since he was a child, of visiting other families in Townsend Street just when they were about to have a cup of tea and a snack, so he was fed wherever he went. To this day he can still list the preferred treats in his neighbours' houses. Visits to the Campbells, for example, had always been especially profitable, because, with four adults in the house, there was always one of them ready to put the kettle on.

So when he decided to diet, there was nothing exceptional or scientific about it – he simply reduced the amount of food that he ate. It is said that one of the secrets to successful dieting is motivation and Hugo was clearly determined, for he got himself down to thirteen stone and stayed that way for several years. 'When I looked at myself at sixteen stone, I thought, this is not going to get the girls, and that's why I went on the diet,' says Hugo. 'I've tried to diet many times since, indeed I'm on one just now, but I never was as successful as that first time.' The lure of the opposite sex can move mountains, or waistlines.

His mother had her own views on the opposite sex: none of them would be good enough for her son. So she kept her eye on him. It was his new-found status as a working man, though, that brought a new dimension to their strong relationship, for with it came the classic parent–child conflict: he wanted to spread his wings but Susie wanted to keep him close. Hugo regarded himself as a young man but in Susie's eyes he was probably still a young boy. He had a job, he was earning money, he was out and about all the time playing music and he was growing popular; the hormones were bouncing. Susie had spent the first sixteen years of motherhood doing all that she was able for her son; she perhaps overindulged him but, small as she was, if necessary she could always wield the wooden spoon to establish who was boss in the house. Now her concerns were about the fact that he was never in the house, he was always late home and she never knew where he was.

It is certain that one of her worries was that with no male role model in the house or in the family, she was moving out of her depth in terms of dealing with the thoughts and behaviour of a growing teenager, and that he might listen and pay heed to others rather than to her. To be fair to Hugo, he wasn't doing anything more than most young men of his age who were working. He was doing the things that he wanted to do, going to his kind of places. None of it was done to annoy Susie; he was just never at home. All Hugo was aware of was that he and Susie were having words more frequently. It didn't occur to him that Susie was worried, for he didn't notice that she was. He doesn't know if her mind ever dwelt on the notion that it was at this stage of his life that a father might have been useful; it was still the case that they did not discuss the matter. He had lived so long without a father that he didn't bother asking and she never raised the issue.

There was an undercurrent now present in their lives, often almost undetectable, but its influence was felt to greater effect than it might have been in other families because the bond between the two of them was so powerful. 'When you channel all your love and care and attention into another human being and that is given back to you, you create strong emotions,' Hugo says. 'Susie and I loved each other dearly but when we had a fight, it was the real McCoy. Just like I have now with my only child, Suzanne – we adore each other but if there's a falling out, stay clear.'

Susie's health had been giving her cause for concern. This was not the same as the problems she suffered when Hugo was a young boy; now she began to suffer some complications as result of high blood pressure. When she let her worries get the better of her, she would get into a cycle of tension and increased blood pressure, the one affecting the other. In her own words, she was becoming bad with her nerves, but what concerned her most was that there was a physical side to it. She couldn't seem to draw on the same energy that had been her standby for most of her life. She had always been robust, but now there were signs of a slight failing. And at the same time, in front of her eyes, her boy was becoming a man, and even if he wasn't aware of it, she could see Hugo was growing away from her.

If there was a time when the two of them could have talked about the past, about her health and her worries for him, it was in these last few years when Hugo was a teenager, but neither knew that Hugo would be married by the age of twenty and that the opportunity to have those conversations was slipping by. In the three years before his marriage, as he grew from teenager into adulthood, there was very little time for chatting. 'Between work, courting and playing,' remembers Hugo, 'I was occupied seven nights a week.' However, he still slipped money under Susie's pillow as he kissed her goodnight and she was still proud that he was able

Susie and Hugo

Susie (second from the left) and the ladies making tea at Saint Pat's Hall

Hugo, as a youngster, with Susie

Susie at the front door of 27 Townsend Street – just as Hugo remembers her

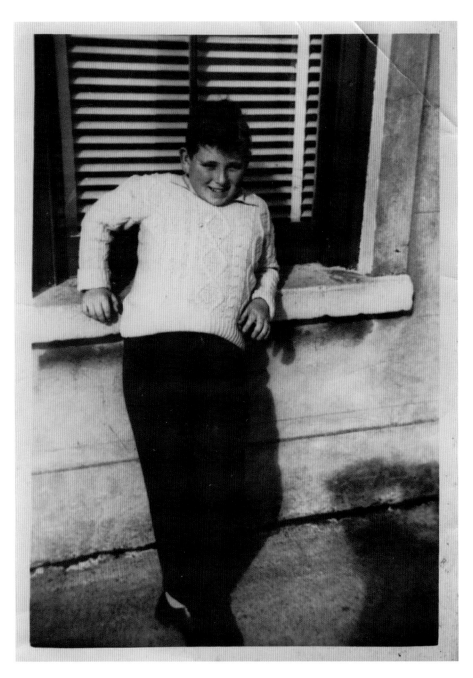

Hugo, lounging against a neighbour's windowsill in Townsend Street

A group of schoolboys whose musical items add much to the enjoyment of the Revue.

Hugo (front row, second from left) with other pupils
from Saint Colman's Secondary School

MIRTH-MAKERS IN STRABANE PANTOMIME

Twelve-year-old Hugh Duncan is "Buttons" and Jack Duffy (right) and Willie Duffy are the "Ugly Sisters" in the annual Strabane pantomime, "Cinderella," now running in St. Patrick's Hall.

Hugo's first review

Outside the Green Café in Lifford with the newly married Porters –
Susie was their bridesmaid

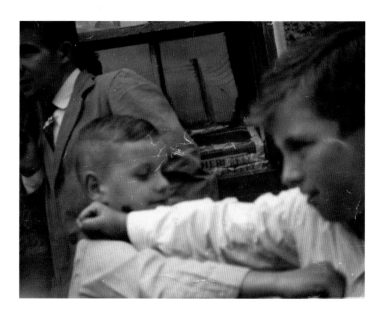

Boxing practice

The young Hugo

Hugo at a practice session with other members of
Dermot Dunn's Ceilidh Band, 1966

Hugo practising the three-chord trick. Joan's brother,
Michael McGuigan, sits beside him.

to entertain people with his music.

Hugo was an apprentice at two jobs. There was the nylon factory, where he took on a new task every six months or so and knew exactly what he had to do in order to get on. There was plenty of potential for advancement. He was a good worker and the other employees enjoyed having him around because he was good crack, which should come as no surprise to those who know him. His way forward was mapped out if he cared to stick to the work he was given and put the years in. But Hugo wasn't entirely happy with his lot, though he couldn't put his finger on why that was.

At the same time, he was serving another apprenticeship, even though it never struck him as such. It was only when he reviewed his career many years later, after he became a professional musician, that he appreciated that those were the days when he was learning his trade in the music business:

> All right, I was earning extra money, making people
> happy, enjoying myself, and although I would have
> practised a lot, mainly learning the words, you don't
> think of it as working towards something, certainly not
> like in the factory. Yet, even though I was so busy
> playing, I don't think that in my teens I ever thought
> seriously about music as a job, something I would do all
> the time.

Having said that, anyone who has played a bit of music will understand why, every now and then, Hugo would allow himself to secretly dream of being like his heroes. During 1966, Joe Dolan topped the Irish charts with 'Pretty Brown Eyes', as did Dickie Rock with 'Come Back to Stay' and Larry Cunningham with 'Lovely Leitrim'. To the sixteen-year-old, these were superstars and Hugo only had to travel down the road to see them, to the Palidrome in Strabane, the Fiesta in Letterkenny and the Butt in Ballybofey.

He wanted to be Joe Dolan. Joe was tall, handsome, successful and a fine singer with a big voice. The first half-hour of any night was spent watching the band as they put on a bit of a show to warm the evening up. The girls might dance together and the boys would pretend they weren't really that interested but, like Hugo, most of them wished they were up on that stage, being Joe.

Hugo was too small ever to hope to be Big Joe Dolan, but he was making progress on other fronts. The diet was bringing results. Having shed the guts of three stone, not only did he have a trimmer figure, but the face was leaner too, and he left the cherub phase to enter what might be described as a more elfin one with his high cheek bones, black hair and what he hoped was a twinkle in his eye. He certainly worked at it, for what he had to practise now wasn't just the three chords and the words; he had to be able to sing and play, and if he was lucky enough to catch the eye of some lassie in the crowd, be able to give her a wink and that wee lift of the head that let her know he'd noticed her. And he had to learn to do all that without making a hames of the song; otherwise he'd look foolish. He got pretty good at the winking.

Although this all sounds slightly frivolous, the serious aspect to it was that this was another lesson in how to win the audience. One evening in a pub in Donegal, Hugo had been impressed by how the singer performing that night engaged with the crowd. Hugo noticed that he made a point of addressing different parts of the song to different people in the room. He was looking them in the eye and reinforcing the notion that he was singing, not for the company, but for each individual in the house. To watch Hugo perform at a dance, concert or broadcast is to observe the same trick in action.

As well as contributing to his musical education, mastering the wink also resulted in the courting business picking up a bit, and just when it seemed he might get good at it, things took an unexpected turn.

Among the hundreds of women working in Adria was a girl from

Newtownstewart, Joan McGuigan. She was pretty, slim and dark-haired, with deep blue eyes. The new trim Duncan was interested immediately and what drew him to the flame even more was that, although he was attracted to her, she wasn't attracted to him. So he set off in pursuit.

In a relatively small rural area, any social occasion tends to attract the same crowd, so as well as seeing him at work, Joan also bumped into Hugo at dances. If she's asked whether she was aware of his attention, she says she couldn't get rid of him, and then after a moment or two's reflection, she'll add, 'And I still can't.' Besides, Joan was some months older than Hugo and knew better than to declare an interest, whether she had any or not. If her intention was to put him off, it didn't work; he kept coming back and eventually she agreed to go out with him. He was seventeen and had his first steady girlfriend.

Even more fortunate, he now had an opportunity to combine his childhood love for the cinema with his courting of Joan. She and her sister, Margaret, were usherettes in Gorey picture house in Newtownstewart, so, when he wasn't out playing, Hugo took himself off to the films, though going there several nights of the week did have its drawbacks. 'For a start, she was working and if I went a few nights in a row, it was the same film,' he says. 'When one of the big popular films came in, it would stay for far longer. I knew every word of *Doctor Zhivago* and if it comes on the TV now, I can turn down the sound and nearly do all the parts myself.' At close on three hours long, he must have spent quite a few days in total watching Julie Christie and Omar Sharif.

He also spent a few shillings on the bus. Until he got his first car, he would get the half past six bus to Newtownstewart and Joan would walk him to the bus stop to catch the last one back home at ten o'clock. If she wasn't working in the cinema, they could either go walking or face her family, who are perhaps better described as a small crowd. 'We'd go to her house, sit down, watch television with her three sisters and seven brothers, get a kiss against the coats in the hall and I would then get the bus back home,' Hugo recalls. 'It was either the pictures, with half the town there, or her front room, with her seven brothers looking on.'

Though at first appearing extremely daunting to the young Romeo, the McGuigan boys, as they were known in the town, accepted Hugo with no reservations. Michael McGuigan and Hugo quickly realised they shared a love of music and became great buddies, with Michael travelling around with him and accompanying him on guitar. For a man who had no family, Hugo was clearly putting himself on track to do the next best thing – get a readymade one.

Susie's disapproving lectures about her son's lateness and absences didn't stop her indulging him when it came to the next required purchase. Fishing rod, bike, drums, guitar and tape recorder had all been bought through Susie's credit system and the first of Hugo's fifty cars was about to arrive the same way.

Many and varied and disastrous are his tales and adventures with cars, including his habit of getting rid of them or writing them off before he'd finished paying for them. At one stage in his life he was paying back loans on three cars, all of which he no longer owned. The first of the long, and often ill-fated, list was an Austin Minivan, bought from a Strabane photographer called Ricky Craig for the grand sum of ninety pounds, the money raised by Susie this time from Strabane Credit Union. It was perfect for carrying his gear – the WEM amplifier, guitar and mike stand – from venue to venue, and perfect also as an alternative courting spot to the Gorey picture house and Joan's sitting room with the seven brothers.

Hugo was a privileged young man indeed, for, in 1968, there were very few seventeen- or eighteen-years-olds running about in their own cars; yet within the year he was on to his second small motor, a Mini saloon, and thus began a pattern of buying that continues to this day.

After eighteen months, Joan and Hugo got engaged. They were both still under twenty and this was a rather more serious turn of events than Wee Susie had bargained for. Her health continued to be a concern. She had suffered a breakdown, which necessitated her being kept in Tyrone and Fermanagh hospital for several weeks. The frequency with which she needed to be cared for increased and, on occasion, Joan would take time off work to nurse her. For the year or so before Hugo's marriage, Susie was in decline. Frequently she was weak and confined to bed, and her blood pressure complications grew more serious. Her full face was now pinched and a lot of the energy was drifting away. The woman who had attended some church service or religious office every day of her life was now struggling to go to Sunday Mass.

Despite the fact that she liked Joan and was content to be cared for by her, Susie was struggling to accept the couple's engagement. Hugo was not surprised by her response:

> It was nothing to do with Joan. If it had been any
> woman, Susie would have felt the same. What she was
> resisting was marriage, not the person involved. I'm not
> even sure if I discussed it with her. I think, as far as she
> was concerned, we drifted towards a point where
> getting married was simply what was going to happen
> next in our lives.

Nevertheless, on the evening of the engagement, a celebration was held at 27 Townsend Street, because that is what happened on such occasions and Susie was always one to do what was expected of her.

In the afternoon, the couple went to H. Samuel's in Derry to buy a ring. Hugo played an early evening gig and then the McGuigan family came to Susie's to toast the engagement. Later that night Hugo decided he'd better fill Joan in on a few details about his family. It seems extraordinary that he hadn't raised the matter before this point but his reluctance to acknowledge or discuss personal matters is typical of his character. He was unaware that Joan had learned many months before about his father's role, or lack of it, in Hugo's life; her brother Michael had given her the details.

That evening Joan and Hugo dandered up the hill to the graveyard lane. This may not seem the stuff of romantic dreams but it's not as bad as it sounds – there are decent views over the town from this spot. He huffed and puffed a bit and declared there was something he needed to discuss with Joan and told her about his father. But before he could offer any further elaboration, she looked at him and said, 'Sure, I already know it anyway.' And that was the end of it.

Although she celebrated the engagement, Susie had always viewed the prospects of any steady relationship with misgivings for two reasons. She had the notion, already mentioned and common to most mothers, that no other woman was good enough for her child, but more than that, she was worried about losing Hugo. He was her only family and the only times they had not been together were when she had been hospitalised.

It was difficult even for Susie to contend that she was losing a son, though, for now that the first floor of the house was habitable, it had been decided that the newly-weds would live with her. So for the moment, then, she was keeping Hugo, although she would have to share him.

On 2 April 1970, Dana entered the British charts with 'All Kinds of Everything' and Hugo and Joan were married in Glen Knock Chapel in Newtownstewart. Margaret was the bridesmaid and Hugo's childhood friend and neighbour, John Sharkey, was best man. Family friend, publican, musician and guarantor for one of Hugo's HP car arrangements, Mickey Christie played the organ, and Father McNicholl conducted the service.

Father McNicholl had been drafted in from Hugo's chapel,

because the priest at Glen Knock was already committed to another engagement, and although a minor matter only on the day, it was to prove a curious coincidence some weeks later.

The reception was held at the Inter County Hotel in Lifford for eighty guests at a cost of one hundred and twenty pounds, and, ever with a great memory for detail, Hugo recalls paying two taxi bills of two and three pounds. The wedding album shows the couple looking relaxed and very happy, with Joan in full-length white dress with veil and tiara and a very trim Hugo. There is a marked difference between this young man and the fuller figure that can be seen in photos from a few years earlier, so it bears out his claim that he shed the pounds to catch the girl. His black hair is short and he's wearing a dark three-piece suit with buttonhole and cufflinks, plus a scattering of confetti. The album also shows Susie in a checked coat that almost dwarfs her. Her face is failed and drawn compared to the photos of her happily pouring tea in Saint Pat's Hall only a few years before. When Hugo took to the dance floor with his mother on his arm, he could not hold back his tears.

Later that day, Joan and Hugo set off in the Austin Mini for their honeymoon in Dublin, though, such was their forward planning, they hadn't booked anywhere to stay. The registration number of the car was KHS 381 D and almost as soon as they drove into the city, they were stopped by the guards. There had been a bank robbery, during which a policeman was shot, and a car with an English number plate would naturally fall under suspicion, for these were the early days of the Troubles and anything unfamiliar was suspect. Having established that the newly married couple had nothing to do with the crime, the guards then took it upon themselves to sort out accommodation for Mr and Mrs Duncan.

On the night of the wedding, shortly after Joan and Hugo had departed for Dublin, Susie fell ill. Although he knew nothing of this, Hugo found he was unable to settle to enjoy the trip; something did not feel right. 'We were supposed to be away for the week,' he says, 'but I had a notion in my head that there was trouble and I knew it was something to do with Susie. It played so much on my mind that I decided we should go back to Strabane after a couple of days.'

Whether it had been some sixth sense or his superstitious nature, when they called into the McGuigan house on their way through Newtownstewart, his fears proved well founded:

> We went into the house, and from the moment we went in there was a strange atmosphere. Everybody was making a great fuss of us, especially of me, and yet I had the feeling that there was something not being said. And then, sure enough, it came out that Susie was in Altnagelvin Hospital and she was not well at all.

She was, in fact, seriously ill. Suffering from malignant hypertension, characterised by abnormally high blood pressure, her body's vital organs were under attack.

On his way to visit Susie, Hugo could not help but dwell on an incident that had taken place in the house a month or so earlier. He and his mother came from a community where experience taught that superstitions are more than just notions and that when portents or signs appear, they are not to be ignored. The incident that had unsettled Hugo and Susie was the appearance of a rat in the house, which, as far as they were concerned, was a sure sign that some trouble lay ahead.

It was common to see rats about the place; they came up from the river at the back of the house. Joan couldn't abide them and went in fear of them when she stayed in the house on her own when Hugo was away. This time, the shock wasn't that a rat had been seen, it was the fact that it was right in the house, in the bedroom.

Susie came to Hugo in a terrible state after she'd gone to lie down one night. She said a rat had run across her head as she lay in bed.

The house was locked up for the night and he was fairly certain that if there was a rat wandering about, he'd have seen it or heard it, for it was a very small house. Besides that, although rats were common, they rarely made it through the yards, for one of the Campbells' fourteen cats would have intercepted them, which was precisely why they were kept. Hugo told his mother to catch herself on, that she was imagining things, but she kept on and on about the rat, so, more to keep her quiet than anything else, he said he would take a look around. Maybe he wasn't as confident as he sounded, for he offered up a short prayer to Saint Martin before he started the hunt, ending with the words, 'If there's a rat in the house, let me find him.'

He left the room and there, sitting halfway up the stairs, was a rat the size of a cat. Suddenly he lit off. Hugo got the poker, went after him, chased him into a room and slammed the door behind him. And the rat was gone. Hugo relates what happened next:

> Now Saint Martin might have answered my prayer, but a rat couldn't just disappear. There was a dresser stood straight up with its back tight against the wall and then I noticed that one of the drawers was just sticking out a tiny bit. The big brute was squeezed into the tiny gap behind, hanging on by its claws. I kicked that drawer with all my strength and there was awful screeching and scrabbling and then it stopped.

That was the end of the rat, but the incident brought an air of foreboding into the house, a foreboding that perhaps had been driven from Hugo's mind by his forthcoming marriage, only to return to his thoughts as he drove to see his mother in hospital. 'I know people laugh at folk like me who are serious about superstition,' says Hugo, 'but I've heard enough and seen enough to know that there are things that are very hard to explain.'

Joan and Hugo set up home in Townsend Street and he travelled to Altnagelvin Hospital each day to visit Susie. Towards the end of the first week, she appeared to rally, but this came to nothing and she went into a sharp decline in the second week, so much so that he spent most of his time with her, coming home only to get a break, change his clothes and grab some sleep.

After sitting up most of the night with her on Wednesday, 15 April, he drove back to the house in Strabane, and having made himself a cup of tea, he gave in to tiredness and lay down on the bed:

> Because it was the middle of the morning and daylight,
> I pulled the blind in the room. It was one of those roller
> blinds. I must have dozed off for about half an hour
> when, suddenly, the blind shot up with the most
> almighty crash. Scared the wits out of me, and I knew
> immediately there was something wrong.

The house had no telephone but he didn't require one to let him know that he was needed and immediately he drove back to the hospital. Susie's damaged organs had simply given up and the life drifted out of her as Hugo sat by the bed, helping her hold a candle in her hand and praying over her.

Susie died on Thursday, 16 April 1970, almost a fortnight to the exact hour after she had stood listening to her son say, 'I do'. She was fifty-nine.

Hugo was in no state to work out what to do, other than phone Dixie Quigley, the undertaker, who, for the next few days, took over his life for him. Susie was carried from her home to the chapel that had rooted her faith all her life and her remains were laid there overnight. Before the lid was screwed onto the coffin, Hugo collapsed in tears across it and so traumatic was the experience of the funeral for him that today, nearly forty years on, he has difficulty talking about it. It remains a raw, emotional time in his memory, as if her death took place months ago rather than years.

The funeral itself had an extraordinary echo from the ceremony that had been conducted for the wedding two weeks earlier: Father McNicholl conducted the service and Mickey Christie played the organ. There was a large turnout for Susie's funeral and no shortage of people to carry her to the graveyard up the road from the chapel. She had friends, neighbours, those who knew her from the church, from Saint Pat's, those she had helped, and she had her son's seven newly acquired brothers-in-law, who cannot have expected that they would need to offer help so soon to the latest addition to their family.

Of Susie's family, there was one only, Hugo, who knows little more about her today than he did nearly forty years ago.

5

What Comes Around

By the time he had reached his twentieth birthday in March 1970, Hugo didn't want for much. He was the apple of his mother's eye, no matter if they had a few differences. He was about to embark on a new stage in life with marriage to Joan. He had a well-paid job at the factory and his music brought him more money and allowed him a certain swagger to his step. This was the comfortable, secure world that revolved around Hugo Duncan, and his marriage wasn't going to change things. The plan had always been for he and Joan to move in with his mother in Townsend Street and he would have continued to be the centre of her world, as well as the centre of his new bride's. 'Susie could have lived for years with us,' says Hugo; 'that's what we expected to happen.'

With Susie's death, Hugo's secure world suddenly disappeared. He was distraught, he was confused, and to some degree he felt betrayed. As he had grown through his teenage years, his relationship with Susie had become more complex and that had brought its own tensions, yet here, at the very moment he was taking a major step forward in his adult life, she had left him.

And with Susie's death, his only secure, intimate source of information about his father and his extended family also disappeared. On the verge of setting out on marriage, Hugo might have been expected to find the time to talk with Susie, but by then he was too preoccupied with a job, playing music, courting and having a good time. Susie died when he was twenty, so the chance never came again. The questions that have cropped up in his mind and the partial answers he's worked out didn't come until he was much older, when only a few of those who had known Susie were still alive. None of those involved in her story is alive today, so what Hugo knows now is the sum of what he will ever know.

That Susie's death signalled a severing of his link to the past was something that certainly didn't register with Hugo at the time: 'I don't think I ever really anticipated sitting down with Susie at some time in the future and talking about our lives. I always had other things to do. It wasn't important enough to me then. Although it's hard for me to say it, there were times when I took my mother for granted.' Joan highlights the fact that there never seemed to be a period when Hugo had time, or made the time, to talk to those who knew his mother and father. There was no impetus to do so after her death and when he became a professional musician shortly afterwards, the pace of life inevitably increased. And to some degree, his control over his life slipped out of his hands. Joan says that even between the two of them, although they have talked about his parents, it tends to have been in the latter years and they never made a determined effort to hunt down information that he would now like to have.

It's only as he considers his life now, as a man in his late fifties, that Hugo knows the conversations with Susie would have taken place some day if she had remained alive; when she would have been less anxious about his future and her health, and he would have been more mature. That is why his sense of loss has, if anything, increased over the decades. He finds it difficult to talk about Susie without a catch in his voice, even tears:

> It's not until you're older that you start wondering
> about some parts of your life that never bothered you
> when you were young. This last twenty years of my life
> have brought so many questions I wish I had the
> chance to ask her, but I can't. So there's parts of her
> life, and mine, I'll never know anything more about.

He knew that Packie McGlynn had eventually married and he clearly knew where his father lived; indeed when Hugo was just turned thirty, he went to see him in Castlederg. He had driven past the house many times but had never summoned up the courage to call in person until one evening he was sitting in the pub with a few friends, one of whom was Gerry McAuley, the neighbour whose house Hugo stayed in as a child when Susie was ill. They'd all put away quite a few drinks, so when the conversation got round to Packie, Gerry, who knew him by sight, agreed to go over with Hugo to the house.

Hugo stayed in the car while Gerry called at the door, only to be told by Packie's wife, Sarah, that he wasn't in. As Gerry came back, a figure walked round the gable end of the house and over to the car. 'He was a big man, over six foot,' Hugo recalls, 'and it was clear he and Gerry recognised each other. Gerry said who I was and that I wanted to talk with him. He put his head in the window of the car, looked at me and then turned and walked away into the house and shut the door.'

It was obvious that Packie wanted nothing to do with them and they drove off, back towards Strabane, but a few miles down the road, Hugo had what he describes as his 'John Wayne moment' and he told Gerry to turn the car round and go back to the house. This time Hugo went to the door and when Sarah answered, he brushed aside her protests that her husband wasn't there and went into the hall:

> He was sitting in a chair in the sitting room. His wife was shouting, 'He's not your father; you don't have a father.' I told him that I wasn't there to take anything, that I didn't want anything from him, and I said, 'All I want to know is, are you my father?' Again he looked at me and then nodded his head and turned away. The funny thing is, I didn't feel anything except a bit

ashamed, because I was drunk and I'd gone barging
into a man's home.

Hugo turned and left but by this time Packie's daughter, Marion,
had arrived. She lived close by and took Hugo into her house,
where, for the first time, he talked with his half sister. Sarah joined
them and they chatted for a while, though, through drink,
confusion and embarrassment, he doesn't remember much of the
conversation:

> I don't know what I expected. It had been bugging me
> for years that I knew where he lived and then, once I
> did something about it, all the energy went out of me.
> It was like walking into a room where you expect to
> recognise something, but everything, everything, is
> unfamiliar and you realise you have no place.

What he does remember from his conversation with Sarah and
Marion confirmed that uncomfortable sense with which he'd left
the house – Packie McGlynn had another life, his own life and his
own family, and Hugo had blundered into it. It didn't matter that
the woman Susie met in the street knew Packie to be the father of
her son. It didn't matter that the children in the playground had
called Hugo by the nickname Pokey. It was now clear that, although
Sarah and Marion knew of Hugo's existence, Packie's relationship
with Susie and the circumstances of Hugo's birth had never been
discussed with them. Just as Susie had, for whatever reasons, shut
Packie out of her life, so too had he consigned Hugo to a time from
his earlier days, long gone.

Hugo maintained a distant contact with Marion, and although
they meet on occasion, their conversation tends to be about their
own families and what they are doing today rather than what
happened in the past. He says she is quite like him, bubbly and

happy to sing a song if given the chance. And they are very similar in another way; they both consign the past to the past, and although she has talked about her father, they have never had a close conversation about Packie nor the family history. What Hugo misses is not the history, it's his mother.

He visited his father once more, when Marion asked Hugo to visit him in hospital, but by then Packie had Alzheimer's disease and wasn't aware of him anyway.

The only other occasion Hugo was in his father's presence was at his wake:

> I stood at the back of the room that day and there were
> so many feelings going through my mind. It's very hard
> to be in that position. You feel guilt on your own side
> and yet you had nothing to with it. I felt guilt and I
> didn't know if it was my fault or whose it was.

Weighing up the sum total of what he knows about Packie and Susie, Hugo is less harsh about his father's absence from his life than might be expected:

> I have no reason to be painting him blacker than black.
> The fact of the matter is that no one truly knows what
> went on and I now take the view that there are three
> sides to the story – Susie's; my father's; and the truth.
> And I'll find out no more about it in this world.

In the midst of his grief and confusion following Susie's death, Hugo had to consider a very practical problem. His diary was filled with gigs and dates. He wasn't sure if he wanted to go back to the music quickly but, on balance, he now reckons that he was probably keener to do so than not. What was worrying him slightly more was how others might view his dilemma. So ten days after Susie died, when Father McNicholl visited the house, Hugo asked him if it would be regarded as a sin if he went back to the playing. He was greatly heartened to hear the priest tell him that neither God nor his recently departed mother could possibly object to him bringing entertainment and pleasure to others.

Indeed, Father McNicholl's encouragement didn't only benefit those who enjoyed Hugo's music; it was a form of therapy for the musician himself, and it also made him aware of something that had been no more than a day-dream previously. 'In the weeks after Susie died, music was definitely one of the things that kept me going,' he says. 'I don't think I had realised till then just how much I wanted it.'

As if to confirm his own inklings and the blessing of the Almighty, Hugo was invited to join the Melody Aces. This wasn't the first band he had been in; as well as Dermot Dunn's Ceilidh Band, he'd already sat in with a number of outfits from the area, including Harry Vance and the Rhythm Aces, Patsy Hart and the Aranville, and Jim McKenna and the Comets. The invitation to join the Melody Aces was significant, however, because, as well as being asked to play bass, he was also expected to share some of the singing. A band's pedigree was determined by the quality of its musicianship and the ability of its key singers to squeeze the most out of any song and hold the attention of the crowd. The Melody Aces already had a couple of fine singers in David Coyle and Shay Hutchinson, and to some fans their reputation as a Strabane band would have been on a par with that of the Clipper Carlton, so the interest in Hugo confirmed that not only did he have the quality of playing to stake a place in an established band, they were also prepared to back him as someone who could make an impact with the punters.

The Aces had a year's dates mapped out in advance, but with a bit of give and take here and there, Hugo was able to keep the day job going alongside his job with the band. Until he was eighteen it had been easy fitting in singing and band work with his job at Adria, because, legally, he could only be put on day shifts. After eighteen, he was expected to fit in with the factory's twenty-four-hour shift pattern, so he was constantly swapping favours with his co-workers. In a place that employed so many workers, there was always someone who had a good reason to swap, but a smaller employer would probably have shown him the door.

Playing with the Aces gave Hugo, for the first time, a whiff of the real music business, one that relied on impressing promoters. These ranged from parish priests to professional backers and the job was to get on the books of as many halls and dance venues as possible, earning return bookings and being part of that scene that was showband entertainment in Ireland at the end of the sixties. Hugo loved it.

Between 1950 and 1980, it is estimated there were close to two thousand Irish bands playing in hundreds of venues across the island. Some were a more or less permanent fixture; others blossomed and then quickly died; there were splits and splinter bands and there was always some outfit that was being re-formed. Variously described as dance bands, showbands, beat groups and Irish country bands, they played the music that provided the backdrop to the age-old dance of flirtation, seduction, love and marriage. The song titles, the singers, the band names and vague memories of dance halls long gone are the stuff of nostalgia, but in browsing through names like the Freshmen, the Platters, the College Boys, the Clipper Carlton, the Miami, Dave Glover, the Royal or Dickie Rock, and trying to pick out the individual faces from snapshots disguised in the hair and fashion and youth of different eras, one thing becomes clear. With the exception of a few performers, such as Eileen King, Philomena Begley, and Margot and Susan McCann, they were all men. Hundreds and hundreds of men, who over the space of thirty years, from around the time of Hugo's birth, were travelling the country, forming bands, leaving bands and writing themselves into future archives; and Hugo was about to become one of them.

It was as if his life had bounced forward after the loss of Susie, and, indeed, one of Hugo's adages is that unless someone is very unlucky, good tends to follow bad, sadness and happiness appear in equal measure, and the circle keeps coming round: 'What's for you will not go by you,' he says.

There was further news too on the home front for Hugo. In the early summer of 1970 Joan announced that she was pregnant. This news didn't strike Hugo as surprising at all; it was simply further confirmation of his sense that there is a balance to everything. It was natural that if a life had been taken away, another would be given.

Only a few months before, Joan had been a single girl, living in a bustling, noisy home, engaged in preparations for her marriage. Now she was an expectant mother, living in a small house with a husband who, when not at work in the factory, was seldom at home because he was on the road. Joan was never under any illusion that she might find a social life in Hugo's world of singing and touring; there was no enjoyment to be had in travelling to gigs and hanging round for most of the evening, waiting for the music to end. It wasn't expected and it wasn't encouraged. If she and Hugo agree on one thing after forty years in the business, it is that neither anticipated any normal social life through Hugo's belonging to a popular band, and they weren't disappointed.

As her pregnancy progressed, Joan increasingly felt alone and she talked with Hugo about him giving up the Melody Aces. He had a secure job at the factory and earned a good wage. It was a discussion to which they returned a number of times and Hugo says that at one point he agreed to give up the band and return to playing weekend solo gigs, but he never put the plan into action. Knowing that Hugo could be awkward if he didn't get his way, it seems likely that Joan eventually decided that he might be worse to live with if he thought he was being denied the opportunity he'd been offered with the band. It was, without doubt, something on which he had set his heart.

In January Suzanne was born. With his wages from Adria and what he earned from the music, Hugo's income was close to fifty-five pounds a week. The average house price in Northern Ireland at that time was around four thousand pounds, a gallon of petrol was thirty-five pence, and you could get a pint for less than ten pence if you knew the right place. So all and all, this was very good money for a twenty-year-old to be bringing in around the town of Strabane.

The conversations he'd had with Joan about maybe easing back a bit as far as the music was concerned might have prompted another man to consider that the arrival of a baby should demand more of his presence at home rather than less. Perish the thought. With the nappy bucket going full blast and his mother probably spinning in her grave, Hugo decided to support his new wife and young family by leaving his permanent employment to join those hundreds of men who were touring the country; he decided to go into music full time.

In retrospect, Hugo admits that, in spite of the arrival of the baby, he still thought the world revolved round him, and he didn't give much thought to how his actions might impact on Joan or anyone else. He now had a genuine taste for the admiration and kudos that came with playing in the band, for singing with the Melody Aces put him in front of crowds big enough to make him feel a touch of the Joe Dolan factor. Throw in the fact that he was about to be head-hunted and it's easy to see how Susie Duncan's wee boy was being led into temptation.

From time to time, he would enter various talent contests, more to see how he would fare rather than being overly interested in winning. In any band he'd been in over the past four or five years, he had been the junior member, and despite the fun he was having with the Melody Aces, Hugo convinced himself that he had settled into more or less the same pattern with them. The truth was that, though he had been given a decent share of the spotlight for a relative newcomer, there was no way two established singers like David and Shay could make more room for him. There was an order of seniority in the bands and if you expressed ambition that didn't reflect the time you had served, you were liable to find yourself looking for a new outfit. Hugo understood this, but he was frustrated: 'I was always the cub. I didn't mind that so much because it had its advantages, but it meant also that you probably had to work that bit hard to get noticed and if I wanted to play a certain song or sing one, there was a bit of a pecking order to go through.'

The talent nights were one way for Hugo to flex his musical muscles.

At one of these competitions Hugo made a big impression with a man called Pio McCann. He was a musician of some standing and influence, and to any regular frequenter of the dance halls, instantly recognisable as the bass player with the Polka Dots, one of those showbands that have become the stuff of legend. Pio did a bit of singing as well and was renowned around the halls for his Fats Domino renditions. He was also on the lookout for a new singer, because the man whose name was synonymous with the Polka Dots, Frankie McBride, was moving on.

The Polka Dots were owned by Barney Curley, a bookmaker from Irvinestown. Barney owned the gear, the outfits and probably the van as well, so, without him, they didn't travel too far. He had created the Polka Dots out of another band called the Claxtons, and ran a number of bands, including one of the best in Hugo's eyes, Brian Coll and the Buckaroos. As well as having a considerable influence on Hugo's destiny, Barney achieved a certain notoriety in 1984 when he decided to sell his Westmeath house in a raffle, with tickets priced at two hundred pounds each. He was a canny businessman but he also had a genuine interest in the music, so any new singer would require Barney's approval, as well as that of the band.

The Polka Dots were a hugely popular band and Frankie McBride had a considerable reputation, not least because he had achieved what so many Irish artists had failed to do: a place in the UK Top Twenty with 'Five Little Fingers' in 1967. It was important that the band members themselves agreed on a new front man who would keep the crowds coming in and the engagement book full. Pio McCann thought that Hugo might fit the bill, so he was invited to an audition with the band. It soon became clear it wasn't just his singing that was under scrutiny.

Hugo is a small man, five feet five inches in the privacy of his bathroom. All the boys who fronted the bands were big, either tall or big shouldered. In other words, they had a physical presence that made them stand out, so that punters at the back could see them through the crowds. This was undeniable logic and sound business sense. 'You have to remember if you were playing to a thousand, fifteen hundred, two thousand,' says Hugo, 'there wasn't much crack if the people who paid the money couldn't see who was singing their favourite song. Brendan Bowyer, Dickie Rock, Joe Dolan – these were all big men.'

Hugo auditioned, and given that he certainly didn't measure up to the required height, he needed to be extra impressive. Pio argued his case. The Polka Dots had been considering a change of direction anyway, and no better time to do it than when Frankie was leaving, so maybe the question of the singer's physical stature didn't matter just as much if there were no doubts he could deliver the repertoire. After four or five years performing on an expanding local circuit, Hugo's popularity was high in Tyrone, Derry, Donegal and Leitrim. Whatever debate there may have been about hiring him, Hugo was asked to join the band as its lead singer on a guaranteed wage of forty pounds per week.

It was with some regret that Hugo told the Melody Aces he was leaving, for he had enjoyed his time with them and he'd known some of the band members since he was a child. The Aces' leader, Johnny Devine, dangled one last carrot in front of him, knowing that Hugo was mad on cars. 'Johnny said they'd get my name put on the insurance and I could drive the van,' Hugo recalls. 'But it didn't sound as good an offer as having my own band.'

The revamped Polka Dots' arrival on the dance hall scene was planned like a military campaign. Greg Hughes was brought in as manager. Greg had been a Gaelic footballing legend as fullback for Offaly, who through his sport and contacts had the ear of a considerable number of promoters and venue owners across the country, not just in the North-West. He was very experienced in the business, most notably with the Times showband, some of whom had been with Joe Dolan's backing band, the Drifters. Joe was still a hero of Hugo's, so as far as he was concerned, if Greg was working with him, the future couldn't be anything but promising.

Hugo, Pio and the band went into rehearsal for two months, while Barney considered the future. He was of the view that not only should the band change direction; with a new singer, they should rechristen the band as well. For a while they were the Big Country and even played a few rehearsal dates in Dublin, but they discovered there was another band trading under that name. Greg was watching them playing one afternoon and suddenly noticed what had been there for all to see: not only did they have one of the shorter lead singers in the business, all the other musicians in the band were bigger than him. The name was obvious, the Tall Men.

So the Tall Men it was, and in the same vein, Pio suggested that they come up with a fond nickname for Hugo, a sort of affectionate by-line that could be used in promotional material. 'What about the Wee Man from Strabane?' someone suggested. 'After all, sure that's exactly what he is.' And that's what he's been known as from that day to this.

It would be Greg's job to sell the band and the Tall Men sat for their first publicity photographs. Though two members are dressed in collar and tie, the pictures capture the band in an informal mode, nothing like the dapper stage presentation they would later adopt. Eight young men, with Hugo clearly the youngest: Pio McCann (bass), Paddy Philips (organ) and his brother Sean Philips (drums), Damien Given (trumpet), Leo Doran (sax), Martin Cunningham (lead guitar), Aidan McPeake (rhythm guitar), and Hugo on vocals. There's a mixture of hair lengths, with a tendency towards long, sprouting sideboards. Hugo sports a waistcoat and sideboards but, as yet, no beard, and still has the lean look to his face that he had on his wedding day.

Almost a year to the day after his mother died, Hugo embarked on his new career, taking the stage in Newtownstewart on Easter Sunday, 1971, as the lead singer of the Tall Men.

6

The Tall Men

Having found a new front man in Hugo and renamed the band the Tall Men, Barney and Greg set about promoting the new group with a focus that any company director and his marketing manager would recognise immediately.

Barney financed the set-up costs, the time for rehearsals, new equipment, publicity and, just as crucially, let it be known to his network of business contacts that he had a new product on the market. And a product is exactly what it was. The place for sentiment and emotion was on the dance floor. As far as Barney and the other promoters and managers were concerned, they had invested in a commodity and their chief concern was maximising the return on that investment. Greg went through his extensive contacts book, made phone calls, called in favours and reminded promoters and agents that he hadn't let them down so far and had no intention of so doing.

Ireland's music entertainment business in the seventies wasn't a haphazard collection of venues, musicians and managers, nor had it been for many years. Though it still relied to some extent on the small halls that were to be found in every town and on local committees keen to put on events, it had become a business, and the rule of business applied.

Communication was important. Sammy Barr at the Flamingo ballroom in Ballymena needed to know how a local band had fared in Roscommon, and equally, Denis O'Mahoney wanted to know which bands from the North might fill his halls in Cork. There was an information network and it included reputations. In any season some bands, or perhaps more correctly, their front men, were gaining or declining in popularity and the manager of a ballroom expecting to pull in a couple of thousand paying customers needed to know this, otherwise he stood the chance of losing money. Oddly enough, knowing who was on the up was also important, for if a couple of shillings more could be charged for a band that everyone wanted to see, the profit margin could increase significantly.

The reputations of the managers and owners of the bands mattered too. Those not in the business of marketing, selling and purchasing may be forgiven for believing that all sorts of shenanigans go on and nobody can be trusted when it comes to money. In the commodities world these goings on are known as 'doing deals' and are based on a constant to and fro of give and take, plus an ongoing assessment as to whether the dealer is getting or giving good value for money. At the end of the day, if the product doesn't come up to scratch, the one who supplies it will find it harder to do a deal on his or her terms next time around.

Greg was trusted. He delivered what he promised. The bands he was associated with turned up on time, played the music that was expected, brought customers through the door and helped the profit margin. Before the Tall Men went on the road, Greg had the band's diary filled up for that first summer and the following year. That meant seven nights a week.

Filling the diary, however, wasn't the only arm of the strategy. Exposure to as wide an audience as possible was essential and for most artists, unless they were lucky enough to appear on television, that meant radio coverage. In 1971 airplay really meant Radio Éireann. There was no station in Northern Ireland playing local music, though from time to time there were ceilidh programmes on the BBC Northern Ireland Home Service. In order to get plays on Radio Éireann, bands had to make records. So almost as soon as the Tall Men began playing, Hugo went into the recording studio.

However, he didn't record with the band. It was the practice, as in the American country music industry, to record with session musicians who lived close to the studios and who were used to playing the material under recording conditions, day in and day out. Studios were rented by the hour, so the faster the work could be done, the more economically the music could be produced. Hugo's first recordings were done with session men, all of whom were professionals and included members of the RTÉ Orchestra. By coincidence, one of those who took part in the session was a new recruit to the recording business, Arty McGlynn, who lived down the road from Hugo and became one of Ireland's most gifted and highly respected guitarists.

Greg organised the recording session, which took place in the Television Club in Harcourt Street in Dublin and was produced by Dermot O'Brien. Dermot came with a list of credentials to which a young singer making his debut in the recording studio could only aspire. He was Ireland's internationally known accordion player, whose string of hits included 'The Galway Shawl', 'The Old Claddagh Ring' and 'The Merry Ploughboy', for which he'd been awarded a gold disc. What's more, he had his own television show and had recorded a Saint Patrick's Day special with Bing Crosby that had been screened coast-to-coast in the States. His production credits included Larry Cunningham, so Hugo was content that he was in good hands.

Because the studio venue was also a fully operational night club, it was unavailable at certain times of the day and Hugo recorded his first batch of songs around three o'clock in the morning, by which stage his voice had almost given up.

No matter who did the actual playing on the recording, the Tall Men's first single was 'I'll be with You Sweetheart in the Spring', a song that ticked many of the required boxes. It is a gentle ballad, with a clear Irish theme and filled with yearning, but RTÉ was a touch sensitive about lyrics in the early years of the Troubles, so although a snippet might be played to accompany information about where the band was appearing, the song was usually faded out before the start of the second verse – 'When all Ireland's wrongs are righted, our hearts will be united'. This fell far short of the band's objective – that having a record would bring lots of airplay; but never mind, it was only a question of recording another single.

The band released 'Dear God', with a B side of 'Another Day, Another Dollar'. 'Dear God' had been a hit for Patsy Cline in 1958 and was composed by V.F. Stewart, who wrote a number of songs for her, including 'Come On In and Make Yourself at Home'. 'Dear God' has a universal theme of human frailty and a striving for the unachievable:

> I go to church on a Sunday
> The vows that I make
> I break them on Monday
> The rest of the week
> I do as I please
> Then come Sunday morning
> I pray on my knees.

It might have been written with Hugo in mind. Better still, it was very successful for him – he got the airplay and the song went to Number One in the Irish charts. Partly because of its eternal theme and partly because it has remained so important to him in terms of his career, it's one of the recordings that Hugo regards with fondness and pride: 'That song is one of the reasons I am where I am today. It has been very good to me over the years.'

It's also the source of one of his favourite anecdotes. Some years later he met a priest down in the south-west of Ireland who told him that he always tried to bear in mind the world his parishioners experienced outside the chapel. He was searching for some device or story that would help his congregation appreciate the need to take what they heard in chapel into their daily lives. The radio was on in the corner of his study and his attention was caught by Hugo singing 'Dear God'. Inspired by the Wee Man from Strabane, he delivered a sermon based on the current chart topper of the time.

Those keen to update their record collections should visit a website called Solid Viper Records. It's based in Chicago and specialises in 'rare vinyl records'. Among its listings under 'Genre: Folk' is the single 'Dear God, 1971, Ireland, center hole intact'. It can be had for $5.79 plus $5 shipping. You can't keep a good man down.

Now that the band had something that could be played on Radio Éireann, the name of the Tall Men became increasingly well known and the band fell into that happy upward spiral where their growing reputation triggered more airplay and vice versa. For the first time Hugo began truly to appreciate that success in the entertainment business depended to a great degree on the commercial interests involved. It was no longer enough for his audience to learn of his next appearance through word of mouth and posters; in order to reach the lucrative all-Ireland market, more sophisticated advertising and promotional strategies were needed. In rural Ireland especially, radio was the medium for the masses and the more airtime that could be commandeered for a product, be it breakfast cereal or a country band, the greater the chance of getting a slice of the market.

Barney ran a variety of businesses and he had the diverse circle of acquaintances that any businessman builds up. One of his contacts was Con Hynes, who managed a string of dance halls known as Associated Ballrooms. These were spread throughout Ireland, so if the manager of a singer or a band could get a successful booking in just one of Con's dance halls, he or she could be fairly certain that further bookings would open up in all the venues run by Associated Ballrooms. Not only that, once Hugo and the band were seen to be clearly in favour with the Con Hynes chain, other owners, promoters and managers would take note and, in turn, seek a bit of the action. In other words, a band previously unknown in

Carlow and its hinterland could rapidly gain in popularity and financial potential, as a result of doing one successful date in an Associated Ballrooms venue.

Radio Éireann was a commercial station, reliant to some degree on the revenue it created from advertising. In the sixties and seventies, modelled very much on common practice in American stations, big advertisers bought airtime in the form of programmes rather than advertisement slots. These were known as sponsored programmes, and Associated Ballrooms had its own regular output on Radio Éireann.

Associated Ballrooms was selling space in its venues, space for entertainment, for dancing and listening to music. It was selling relaxation and romance. In order to entice people into that space, it used bands and singers, so the more familiar and appreciative the clients were with those who played the music, the better the business. On its radio shows, therefore, the company profiled the key bands in its stable, and through Barney's connection with Con, the Tall Men featured prominently in the fifteen-minute slot, broadcast late on a Thursday night. Just in time to capture the weekend dancers. For Hugo, this was a huge personal boost:

> Yes, people had televisions but after ten o'clock at night
> there was nothing to watch. In every corner of the
> country, the radio was the late evening entertainment
> and I could sit in Strabane, listening to myself, knowing
> there were thousands doing the same in Limerick,
> Cavan, Kinsale; stick a pin in the map and they'd be
> listening, some of them in the certain knowledge I'd be
> singing down the road in a week or two. Suddenly, we
> could play anywhere in Ireland.

The Tall Men were not a country band. There was a fair sprinkling of country material and Hugo already enjoyed singing songs by the likes of Buck Owens, Charley Pride and Tom T. Hall as well as Irish standards such as 'The Old Dungannon Road' and 'Take Me Back to Castlebar', but like any band playing a variety of venues, they knew how to mix the song list. This included a sprinkling of rock and roll, and Pio McCann excelled at the more rhythm-and-bluesy style of singing. The band also had brass players, which extended even further the styles and arrangements they could play.

The music was played in sets of three songs or tunes, often following the pattern of three quicksteps, followed by three foxtrots and then a set of three waltzes. There was no running order of tunes for the evening; they had a list of a couple of hundred numbers that could be called at any stage in the performance. Pio or Paddy Philips would call out the tunes and their selection would take into account what the crowd was like on the night, whether they were good dancers, the number of couples as opposed to singles seeking partners, the peculiar mood and atmosphere that accompanied each venue. The band was well drilled and well rehearsed, so that its members didn't waste time trying to remember which key to play in or the opening lines of a song, and this was based on hard work.

It was often the case that the Tall Men would get their gear set up well in advance of starting time and rehearse before the crowd began to drift in. Song medleys, in which several popular tunes are joined together, always received extra attention, for a well-delivered medley could keep the dancers on their feet for longer than a single tune, as well as provide an opportunity for the band to show off its skills. They also worked at presentation songs, which were designed to entertain the crowd before the serious business of the evening got under way, or to be played in a sort of cabaret slot at some stage during the evening. These often featured more complex arrangements, with players swapping instruments and giving solo performances.

So playing the booking was only one aspect of a band's routine work, solid rehearsal was part and parcel also and each member was expected to work out and learn new material in their own time, so that when they came together, there was no hanging about while others caught up.

Hugo and the boys also had to look after their wardrobe. Though the Tall Men never went in for the more flamboyant outfits favoured by some bands, their suits were tailor made in a mixture of colours – black, light blue with beading; brown with dark brown satin lapels. They were well cut and well made, reflecting the style of the time and delivering Greg's marketing tack that this was a band that didn't need to show off, this was a band that had class. It was from this time that Hugo began to fancy himself in waistcoats and developed a taste for three-piece suits, as befitted his status as a lead singer.

Hugo was becoming better known but he wasn't well known yet; he certainly wasn't famous. To achieve that required years of sustained success on the circuit, like Joe Dolan, or an appearance on television. Fortune smiled on Hugo and once again it was helped by the business contacts of those close to him. Greg had a strong contact in RTÉ television, who was persuaded to let Hugo appear on *Reach for the Stars*, a major music talent show.

This wasn't Hugo's first flirtation with the medium. When he was ten or eleven he had travelled to the Ulster Television studios on the Ormeau Road in Belfast to audition for *Tea Time with Tommy*. This local entertainment show was hosted by Tommy James, who played tunes on his piano for viewers' birthdays and anniversaries, and, with his trio, accompanied amateur performers as they did their turns. In some ways it was an odd programme to come across in a local schedule, for Tommy spoke with an English accent and the theme tune, 'Tea for Two', reflected nothing of the place in which it was made, but this didn't seem to matter, for it was enormously popular with the Northern Ireland audience.

Hugo's name was probably put forward by the school; it certainly wasn't his mother, because although she delighted in his performances, she never pushed him to the front. Even in later years, Susie and he never discussed ambition; she seemed to be happy with her lot and content that he had found himself a secure job in the factory. Those moments when he aspired to being Joe Dolan or Brian Coll, he kept to himself.

Susie and Hugo travelled to Belfast by train along with Joe and Peggy McManus, two of their neighbours. At Havelock House, they met Tommy, who struck up the opening bars of Hugo's number in the key of A. The youngster was used to singing it in the key of D, so he was now trying to sing the song in a low pitch that he wouldn't be able to reach until Nature took her course in a year or two. Unfortunately, he was so overcome with his surroundings that he didn't have the wit to ask Tommy to start again in the right key. Disaster ensued and they took the train back to Strabane convinced that Hugo's one chance to be on the box had been blown.

Ten years later, Hugo didn't make the same mistake at RTÉ's Donnybrook television studios.

Even given our familiarity with recent series like *X Factor*, *Fame Academy* and *Pop Idol*, it's difficult to imagine the large numbers of people who watched big television entertainment shows nearly forty years ago and, hence, the enormous excitement created by the artists who appeared on screen. There was nothing approaching the wall-to-wall television music and entertainment available to today's viewers, where entire channels are devoted to endless music videos. So whenever RTÉ invested in any of its television entertainment strands, these had to achieve maximum impact for the broadcaster, the advertisers and the viewers.

There was another powerful catalyst in the whole entertainment broadcast mix in Ireland at the start of the seventies. Hugo was turning professional at a time when, north and south of the border, Ireland's interest and excitement in home-grown singers was probably at its peak. Some of the biggest names in the music business had acquired almost legendary status, and with the decline in the showband boom only a year or two away, this is when they would stand tallest in the memories of most fans. Larry Cunningham, Brendan Bowyer, Butch Moore, Dickie Rock and Joe Dolan were still household names, and no one could see any reason why they and their ilk would not continue to pack the dance halls for another decade.

As if to confirm the optimism, in March 1970 Dana won the Eurovision Song Contest. Some of the big hitters had already come close for Ireland: Dickie Rock and Pat McGeehan, better known to some as Pat McGuigan, father of world boxing champion, Barry, had both managed fourth place, and in 1967 Sean Dunphy took second spot behind Sandie Shaw and could console himself with the knowledge that at least her song, 'Puppet on a String', was written by a man from Derry.

Dana was welcomed home by ten thousand well-wishers. She narrowly avoided being made a saint then and there and she gave RTÉ a headache, a welcome one, but a headache none the less. Apart from her instant and enduring stardom, the most direct result of her win was that Ireland would host the Eurovision Song Contest in 1971 and the national broadcaster of the Irish Republic was to play broadcast host to all its colleagues and peers across Europe. The entire country was in spasms and so was RTÉ, because this was to be its first colour outside production and there could be no bigger stage on which to do it. Then, as if things couldn't get any better, it turned out that the UK was to be represented by yet another girl from the North – Warrenpoint's Clodagh Rodgers, who was strongly tipped to win.

For the record, Clodagh came fourth with 'Jack in the Box', Angela Farrell was eleventh for Ireland with 'One Day Love' and Séverine won for Monaco with 'Un Banc, Un Arbre, Une Rue'.

Hugo certainly hadn't picked a bad time to throw his singing hat into the Irish show business scene. *Reach for the Stars* was both a talent contest and a showcase for young talent. There were only

BBC, ITV and RTÉ television programmes to watch, so if artists could grab a space on a show that was in any way popular, their profiles shot up. Hugo appeared three times in the show in as many months. He was twenty-one, looked younger, and every time he was voted through to the next round, it gained him more publicity. He nearly won the whole thing but not quite: 'I was runner-up to Fran O'Toole, God be kind to him, but I didn't mind because I knew he was going to be a star,' says Hugo. 'He was tall and slim and fair-haired. I was shorter and less slim, though I'd plenty of hair, black and curly.'

However, he almost managed to cock it up before he began, just as he had at his first attempt at television all those years ago. The band dropped him off at the studios in Dublin and headed down country to their next date, where Hugo would join them later. As the van disappeared round the corner he suddenly realised that all his gear was in the back, including his fancy suit, which was just the dog's business. There was none of the convenience of a mobile phone in those days, so he went off in search of the wardrobe department and eventually made his debut wearing someone else's woollen polo-neck sweater. If he hadn't lost the weight already, he'd have shed a pound or two under the studio lights that evening.

Coming second didn't worry him. Apart from the fact that he believes the best man won anyway, he had been forewarned. The Tall Men were playing an outdoor event several weeks before the final and among the thousand or so packed into the marquees were some RTÉ staff who knew Hugo from the show and told him that the winner and runner-up had already been decided upon. Far from being annoyed at this revelation, he looked forward eagerly to his new status as runner-up, and as it turned out, his young looks attracted a backwash of sympathy from viewers and his reputation round the halls rose in equal measure. So he never regretted or felt he lost out by not winning the contest.

What he regrets is that his mother wasn't there to see that he was making his mark.

Between 1971 and 1975, Hugo released ten singles, seven of which ended up in the Irish Top Twenty. He and his band were on equal footing with any one of their contemporaries. He was capable of drawing a thousand, or fifteen hundred, paying customers, sometimes more, and he could do this far away from his regular stomping grounds in the North-West, where his ability to deliver the product was undeniable.

Several years ago he presented one of his radio outside broadcasts from a steam traction rally in Ballymena and unexpectedly met up with an old acquaintance from Cork, Denis O'Mahoney, who ran the Lila ballroom in Enniskean. Hugo chatted with Denis on air and started to reminisce about the old days, asking him how many people would have come to a Tall Men gig in the Lila. Denis was a bit cagey at first, but once the two of them had reassured each other that the tax man wouldn't be listening, indeed would long ago have given up interest, he said, 'Hugo, if you didn't do two thousand, you wouldn't be back.'

Hugo and the Tall Men once did five nights in a row.

7

Playing by Night
and Pubbing by Day

The Rolling Stones drummer Charlie Watts, a man not above playing the odd country song himself, was asked to reflect on life with one of the world's most famous bands. He pondered for a moment and then replied: 'Basically it feels like we spent five years recording and playing, and thirty-five years hanging around waiting for something to happen.'

Hanging around waiting for the next gig is one thing that Charlie and Hugo have in common. It doesn't matter if the hanging around is done in a private jet or a Volkswagen van, a hotel suite in Buenos Aires or a tearoom in Bundoran, backstage at Wembley Stadium or the Fiesta in Letterkenny, it's still hanging around. When the real job of work doesn't begin until eight, nine or ten o'clock at night, there are a lot of hours in the day to put in. After the initial thrill of spending half a day driving to the Cloudland ballroom in Rooskey, County Leitrim, even the travelling loses it edge and becomes a bore.

Having too much time on their hands has been the plague of musicians since they were first paid to play. Most working people are expected to attend their place of work and stay there for most of the day, so that they look as if they're working even if they're not. Except when they're practising or playing, musicians don't have to be anywhere. If they're focused on a hobby, they have plenty of time to fish, play golf and keep fit, but it usually has to be on someone else's course or in some other gym, for they're rarely at home. But it's probably an even bet that they will fall victim to temptation and devote their free time to indulging themselves – often to excess, if the better stories are to be believed.

In his spare time, Hugo practised his drinking.

It was not the music business that introduced Hugo to alcohol. Since his teens he had taken a drink and moved in the company of those who did. The culture of drinking in Ireland goes hand in hand with socialising, sport, family events and entertainment.

Tales and jokes have always been told about 'the wee drunk man' and, should the wee man's drinking become a problem, the stories tend to be prefaced with, 'Ach, God help him all the same'. One of Hugo's favourite film characters is Michaleen Oge Flynn played by Barry Fitzgerald in *The Quiet Man*. Michaleen personifies perhaps how Irishmen fondly regard themselves: eloquent, quick-witted, entertaining, and having an easy relationship with alcohol. Hugo certainly felt that when he was relaxed, those around him were bound to feel the same:

> When I was on the drink, the crack was great. When you're like that and you think you're having fun, you assume that everyone else is having fun too. You don't for a second imagine that others can't be enjoying it. The truth is, you don't bother to ask yourself and you know there's no point in asking anyone close to you, your wife for instance, for you know you won't believe them if they say something you don't want to hear.

From his early teens, Hugo was used to men drinking. In a small rural town it would be difficult for him to grow up in ignorance of the fact, especially when he roamed so freely round Strabane. Although he grew up with older men around him, he had no single male role model, but he makes this no excuse, for he reckons that as many men followed their fathers into drink as were turned against it. In Scobie's bar he continued his childhood pattern of helping out and doing odd jobs, serving and chatting with the regular customers and observing the ease with which conversation and laughter flowed. Before he began playing in bars with his guitar and three-chord trick, he'd been sitting in with various ceilidh bands in local pubs and hotels, so the world of drink was familiar to him.

All in all, his attitude to drink as a young man was the same as many others his age. It was enjoyable, fairly harmless and may even have been viewed as a rite of passage in growing to manhood: 'That's wee Susie's boy, young Duncan, can take a drink, plays a bit of music as well. He's good fun now.' He felt that in a way he was part of something; there was a recognition that he existed. Drinking made life just that bit easier. His mother warned him from time to time about the ease with which one drink led to another, but he paid little attention, for he could see no harm in it.

Joan knew that Hugo drank when she married him but thought there was nothing unusual in a man taking a drink. She knew that playing music involved a lot of crack and was usually accompanied by a drink or two but, again, there wasn't much to get fussed about.

After their marriage, Hugo's drinking started to increase, yet it was still nothing that he and his fellow regulars would have found need to comment on. The night before his daughter's birth, he toasted the imminent arrival with his friends in the pub, and next day, he celebrated Suzanne's arrival with more friends in another pub; but not before he'd been to the hospital to visit Joan and her child. This was accepted practice for new fathers in those days. The only observation Joan made was that he seemed to be in the pub a lot.

At the time of Suzanne's birth, preparations were well under way to launch the Tall Men. With the Melody Aces, Hugo had already been playing more dates away from home than Joan was happy with, and once the new band went on the road, he was away more than ever. As mentioned earlier, that summer in 1971, when the Tall Men were first established and Suzanne was born, Hugo played seven nights a week.

The records, airplay and television appearances throughout that year and on into 1972 meant that more and more of those dates tended to be much further away from Strabane than had previously been the case. These included not only the far south of Ireland but also England. In 1974 the band topped the bill at Jim Aiken and Barney Curley's Saint Patrick's Day celebration concert at the Royal Albert Hall, and they were capable of packing in over two thousand on a Monday night at an Irish club on the Holloway Road in London. This was a pattern of travelling that accompanied the band's increasing popularity between 1971 and 1974.

With every successful date and each new venue conquered, there were more people who wanted to spend time with the band, chat to them, go out with them and buy them a drink. With every long trip away from home and the hours of every extra day and night to fill, there was more time to spend in a hotel bar or friendly pub and there seemed to be no shortage of new friends to keep Hugo company. As a consequence, by the time he'd spent two years with the band, Hugo entered a phase of his life that is defined simply by the years on the drink rather than the bands he played with or the places he played. They all just rolled together into one long binge and he defines the era as the decade stretching from 1973 to 1983 and being at its worst towards the end of the seventies.

Joan reckons the decline began almost as soon as it was clear that Hugo and the Tall Men had a success on their hands. 'Once he began to do well, he went downhill,' she says. She was a young bride and a new mother living in a small terraced house who was scared to go beyond the back yard because of the rats that came up from the river. Ever since Hugo had recounted the tale of the rat that came into the house before his mother died, Joan had a terrible fear of another one getting in. When he attempted to reassure her by pointing out that the neighbours were always there when he was on the road, she wasn't much impressed. It was all right for him, he had grown up with these people, had known them since he was a child, but as far as she was concerned, they were old folk with whom she had very little in common. After all, she was a young woman, used to a bustling, lively and, above all, youthful family in a house that was always filled with chat and gossip.

By the early seventies also, the Troubles were affecting all parts of Northern Ireland, and Strabane was suffering its full share. Amongst many incidents in 1971 there was rioting that continued into the next year, when the town hall and the customs post were blown up, and in 1973 the town's Abercorn Hotel was bombed. Joan would have been constantly aware of flares of trouble, both further up and down the street from the house.

So, by any stretch of the imagination, Joan was very much on her own. She simply says: 'For the first fifteen years Hugo wasn't here, playing by night and pubbing by day.'

Of course Hugo was aware of the difficulties Joan faced and he knew that at times she was very unhappy with her lot, but as the cycle of playing and drinking grew ever more relentless he told himself that there wasn't a great deal more he could do. Besides, the music was now his only source of income, and as with any job, they both had to take the rough with the smooth. If that included a lot of time of travelling, spent in the company of acquaintances and fans, then that's what had to be done. 'I thought I was enjoying myself, and when it wasn't enjoyment, I still told myself that it was,' Hugo says. 'You always tell yourself that you're not really doing any harm. The truth is that you convince yourself there is no problem in the first place.'

There is no doubt that Hugo regarded the social side of his drinking as good fun. He loved being part of a crowd, one of the boys, and was determined that everyone in the company should enjoy themselves. This is not out of character; Hugo often says that he likes making people smile. To watch him interact with the crowds at any of his outside broadcasts is to see a man who is totally focused on engaging with individuals in the audience, sharing the crack and listening to their stories, and the response from them shows that they know that that relationship is authentic, if the smiles on the faces of those pressed around him are anything to go by. Even those with scant reason to smile receive the same warmth and understanding as he reads out a note handed to him: 'Would Hugo say Happy Valentine's Day to Isobel. It's the first Valentine's Day since her husband died. Of course I will, Isobel, and everybody here sends you their love and God bless.'

It's part of his make-up that Hugo doesn't want people to be sad, and if he can help, he will. So in the bars of Ireland, Scotland, England, and a few in New York, he would buy drink for everyone, so that they would be happy and he wouldn't have to leave. His manager, booking agent and long-time friend, Paddy Bradley, recalls an occasion when the venue they were playing had laid on free drink, but such was Hugo's urge to be with people, he was in the bar next door buying drink for everyone.

Once established, the pattern was monotonous. Hugo would define a good day as one when he went into the bar in the morning, then maybe had a doze at lunchtime and on to more drink in the afternoon. A bad day was just as good, it was just harder to kick-start, 'You'd get up in the morning feeling very sick but you'd have a few drinks and then you'd begin to feel a bit better,' he says. 'From that point on I'd drink before, during and after being on stage.' The really bad days were those when he would order his first drink and then study it for a quarter of an hour or so before plucking up the courage to knock it back. The second was always easier.

For a man who was so much under the influence, he recalls most of the bad times and almost all of the trouble he landed in, and remembers many of the incidents in great detail. He whiled away an afternoon in Bantry, County Cork, drinking and playing poker, and by the time somebody, probably Pio, suggested it might be an idea to get ready for that night's show, he was totally gone. But he can paint a vivid picture of the shower he took before the performance:

I couldn't be bothered taking my trousers off, so I just got into the water, trousers and all. I slipped on the soap and fell down on my backside and the bottle of Pernod I had in my hip pocket smashed and the glass cut me. There was blood running down the plug hole, drink running down the plug hole, and the smell of the aniseed! I just sat there with the water running over me and all I could do was laugh! Mind you, I was never able to face Pernod after that!

For a long time, many years indeed, Hugo was able to maintain his professional career as well as the drinking, but inevitably the effects of the habit found their way onto the stage. Although he always had drink with him when he was performing, things had come on a long way from the time when it might just have been a loosener to help get him into the entertainment mode. 'I was playing one night in Glasgow,' he recalls, 'and I met a boy who had a pub in Downings in Donegal, so I spent the afternoon drinking treble vodkas with him. By the time I climbed onto the stage that evening I was as drunk as I've ever been.' So drunk that he couldn't find his suit, so made his entrance dressed in his jeans, which simply wasn't the done thing. He sang 'The Town I Love so Well' and then decided to sing it again, at the end of which he was physically hauled off the stage and locked in a dressing room with a bouncer on the door under strict instructions not to let him out till the show was over. The band had to do the gig without him.

By the time Hugo's drinking and behaviour had reached this stage, the band was no longer the Tall Men. In common with many outfits, after the first two or three years together, the personnel gradually changed as other opportunities arose or individual members fell out with each other. Musicians were constantly being poached from one band to another; after all, this was how Hugo had ended up as singer with the Tall Men in the first place. This natural turnover, coupled with Hugo's increased drinking and his continuing insistence that he was the attraction for the people who came to hear the band, meant that by the end of 1975 it was no longer Hugo Duncan and the Tall Men, it was just Hugo Duncan.

There was no problem getting a band, however. Several backing bands were put together over the next few years and Hugo was quite happy with this arrangement, for he believed that as long as he was the lead singer, the star draw, the punters would still turn out and the bookings would come in; therefore, how he behaved had little to do with the business side of his life, indeed it wasn't anybody's business other than his own. As far as he was concerned, his drinking didn't come into the equation, for no one was going to sack the lead singer. There may be truth in that, but audiences and promoters reach a point where they won't take any more if they're regularly getting performances that are below par.

In moments of complete exasperation, Con Hynes, who had bought the Tall Men from Barney in the mid-seventies, had told Hugo that he'd see him back sewing buttons on shirts. Yet even then Hugo hadn't seen what was coming. A bit too smart for his own good, he pointed out to Con that he'd have difficulty packing him off back to the shirt factory, because he'd never worked there in the first place – it was a hosiery factory. It's hard not to sympathise with Con and his growing frustration with the singer; he didn't sack Hugo, he simply washed his hands of him. By the late seventies, Tony Loughman and Brian McNiff, Hugo's record managers, were referring to Hugo openly as 'Drunken Duncan'. In the end, Tony gathered the dozens of expensive colour posters that advertised Hugo's forthcoming appearances and gave them to Paddy Bradley. 'Take them, Paddy,' he said. 'Take them and take him too. You're welcome to him.'

Hugo was losing business contacts, losing goodwill, and like anyone working in the entertainment business, he needed people to be acting on his behalf and in his interests rather than ignoring him and transferring their efforts to potential rivals searching for the same gigs. In losing that support, he also lost the infrastructure that took care of technical gear and transport, matters with which he had never had to concern himself. There were plenty of musicians available but Hugo had no van and no PA system. One way round this was to hire bands that played small, local circuits, for they were always looking for a few extra dates and they tended to have their own amplifiers and van, but they had no need to feel any allegiance towards Hugo and as soon as a better offer came up, they'd be away.

By the start of the eighties, bookings were drying up: no one wanted a singer who'd turned up drunk on the last couple of occasions. Even Paddy Bradley came to a day where he could see no point in putting any money into another record deal, because he knew it would be money down the drain. And this was the true low point of Hugo's singing career: bookings were dropping because of his behaviour, so he could no longer even rely on his ability to hire regular musicians and bands, for they would be looking for five or six dates per week and he could now offer only a couple. He was at the mercy of those who might agree to give him a gig or two and those who might play with him if they had nothing better on.

Hugo's notion that he was untouchable, that he would always get through, applied equally to life away from the stage. During his years of drinking, he still drove and it is something of a miracle that although he was the cause of several serious accidents, he never hurt or killed anyone. He himself was extraordinarily lucky to walk away from some of the crashes. On one occasion, still resplendent in a green three-piece suit, he left a gig in Pomeroy, County Tyrone, around two o'clock in the morning. He was very drunk and he drove home the forty-odd miles alone. When he got to Strabane, he remembers the car bouncing off the kerbs, hitting a two-foot wall, turning over and landing on all four wheels, looking as if it had just been parked. It had landed in the forecourt of a petrol station and, realising that it could still be driven, Hugo headed off to see if

McCrossan's pub was still open. It was now around four in the morning. Getting no joy there, he decided it might make more sense to go home, and it was only when he arrived there that he realised he and his green suit were covered in blood. Joan, who was convinced he was bleeding to death, roused the next-door neighbours, Biddy and Willie, and Hugo was taken into their house to be tended to. His cuts eventually required hospital attention and sixteen stitches to get him back together again, but, in the meantime, his activities had been noticed and it wasn't long before two policemen came knocking on Biddy's door.

'Has this man been drinking?' enquired one officer in that tone that makes everyone aware that he knows exactly what is going on but might as well go through the formalities anyway.

Biddy's riposte was as quick as a flash. 'Of course he has, Constable. Sure look at the state of the poor man. Willie here's been giving him brandy for the shock.'

If Hugo was totally irresponsible in driving with drink, he also appears to have got away with it, due in part to a different social attitude thirty years ago. At the time Hugo was drinking seriously, it was regarded as the norm to drink and drive, and the declaration that the licence had been taken away would have been met with general sympathy and a lot of bad mouthing of the police and courts alike. But another factor to be taken into account was Hugo's fame. Quite simply, he got away with things because his face was known. Today, if the face is recognisable and the behaviour is deemed scandalous enough, it's an immediate passport onto the pages of a newspaper. But at that time, the notional headline 'Drunk Country Singer Drives Car' would not have been considered startling by any means.

The police knew him; even the British army on the checkpoints knew him. The attitude was best summed up by a local policeman's response when he came across Hugo drunk in the town. He said: 'Hugo, I should be asking you for your autograph, not looking at you like this. Now get away home.' Hugo doesn't know if the full import of the policeman's remark struck him at the time, for he was more used to people laughing off his behaviour and asking for his autograph. When today he recalls the incident and the officer's words, he almost winces at the notion that this man thought he was nothing but a loser.

Did Hugo wise up?

> I don't know what made me come off the drink. It was no single thing; it certainly wasn't the hangovers, for they were just part of the daily routine. It wasn't my health, for though I often felt bad through the drink, oddly enough it was a time in my life when I never bothered with my health. It wasn't the work because I always muddled through and even when it started to dry up I don't think I cared. And I can't say it was because of my family because if that was the case, I'd have wised up many years before then.

There were several incidents that, taken together, may have triggered Hugo's decision to stop drinking. Some years earlier, Joan and he had moved into a council house at Innisfree Gardens, further up the Head of the Town from Townsend Street. This was an estate that had several entrances and exits and could also be approached easily from the back, away from the main road; hence it was a perfect area for the hijacking and stealing of cars, and Hugo, along with many neighbours, had had a vehicle pressed into service by those who wanted to transport explosives or carry out a job somewhere.

At a time when he could no longer raise credit – no one would take the risk – a friend, Patsy McGillion, managed to get him HP on a Ford Fiesta, transport that was essential if he wanted to stand any chance of fulfilling the few bookings he had managed to secure. But, as Hugo recalls, he didn't have the car for long:

A friend of mine was staying at the house and we were expecting his brother to call, for we were going to the pub – where else? I heard this knocking at the back door, which was lying half-open, and I thought it was him. So I went over and kicked the door and shouted, 'Get away out of that!' Next second, a gun came round the door frame and this boy behind it. 'We need your car,' he says. 'Certainly,' I said. And that was the last I saw of the Fiesta.

A bomb was placed in the back of the car and driven to Strabane courthouse, where the explosion wrecked the Fiesta and broke a windowpane in the building. Needless to say, the experience rattled Hugo and Joan and he didn't need her to remind him that the reason they were living where they did was because he couldn't be bothered to provide properly for his family.

Some time later, after Patsy had been able to arrange further HP on a van and trailer, Hugo's luck with drinking and driving ran out. On 13 September 1983 he was stopped by the police, discovered to be well above the limit, and charged. Although it would be many months before his case would go to court, as far as he was concerned, he was done for and faced the prospect of having to pay, not only the musicians, but now someone to do all the driving. He was already having to play small solo gigs to help finance those with the band, because, as well as spending much of the earnings on drink, Hugo was an appalling housekeeper, who could never quite work out how he'd managed to get paid for an engagement, yet by the next day had no cash with which to pay the band.

Drinking was making life complicated. It was a different matter when he had people to look after him, but things were becoming a bit of a mess, as he admits: 'After I was caught in September, I never said I would give up the drink, but I did think, for the first time, that maybe it wouldn't be a bad idea. I decided to drink for the next

three months – till Christmas – and then see how I felt about it.'
Now, there's a man who knows how to get his priorities right.

A third factor was indeed his health, even if he wasn't aware of
it playing on his mind at the time. Hugo suffers from diverticulitis,
the symptoms of which are abdominal pain, nausea and vomiting,
which can lead to very serious illness. For years he has been advised
to increase his fibre intake and reduce the amount of fat and salt
that he eats, advice that he continues to ignore, though he is only
too ready to reach for the painkillers. 'A really bad attack, which I
would still get, can leave you doubled over in pain and I remember
them being so bad around that time in 1983 that I'd pray to Our
Lady that if she'd only do something for the pain, I'd eat properly,
behave myself and stop the drinking,' he says.

Although it wasn't the drink that caused this condition, it
encouraged the very diet that made it worse – salt, sugar and fats
with no fibre – for, as anyone knows who has been on a good night
out, the body craves such food in the form of Ulster fries, bacon
butties, steak sandwiches, all accompanied by lots of butter and salt.

Thus, while Hugo claimed during his years of drinking that, other
than the odd hangover, it did him no harm, in the end he couldn't
ignore the fact that he suffered serious pain and that perhaps the
drink didn't help.

And then perhaps it had begun to filter through to the decent
man inside the drunk that his wish for the whole world to enjoy
itself excluded the one small group that most wanted it; his family.

8

Second Chance

Early on in his drinking career Hugo quite rightly grasped that he didn't want to hear common sense talked to him. He didn't want to be reminded of responsibility, because that would only stop the party. The person most likely to talk common sense to him was Joan but he had convinced himself that she had little to worry about. Yet he was never at home and he knew that she frequently despaired and took herself and Suzanne off to stay with her family in Newtownstewart; and he knew that others, including a local priest, Father Carlin, had tried to talk sense to him on her behalf. Even in the years he was undoubtedly at his peak as a singer, when radio and television appearances easily came his way and he had records in the Irish charts, he and Joan could never afford to buy their own house. They lived in rented accommodation in Strabane, because everything Hugo earned was spent on drink. When he bought friendship in the bar, he bought for everyone in that bar, not once but over and over again. 'I never had a penny,' he says. 'I drank everything. I'd send Joan downstairs before me in the mornings so that she could get the bills the postman delivered and then hide them somewhere so that I couldn't see them.'

And until her daughter was fourteen, Joan not only had no money, she didn't have Hugo either. Suzanne knows that her father's memories of her childhood are scant and scattered and she knows that he has spent the rest of his life trying to repay her for that. He'll continue to do this till the day he dies. Half the town knows that he was never there. Hugo remembers how, some years ago, after the birth of Suzanne's first child, the proud grandfather was wheeling the pram round the shops in Strabane:

A woman who knew me all her life came over to
admire the baby and she says straight into the pram,
'It's well seen he wheels you round the place, son, for
he sure as God never wheeled your mother.' And she
gave me that look that means nothing is forgotten.

What his family had to put up with for years conditioned them to
living their lives in a fashion that could be constantly and instantly
shifted. Those who live with people dependent on drink or drugs say
that they are constantly alert to behaviour patterns and mood
swings, that their antennae are always twitching. They also know
that an alcoholic can easily delude himself into believing that he
has become a reformed character, so it's hardly surprising that
neither Joan nor Suzanne paid much attention to Hugo's
announcement that he was giving up the drink.

'I had my last drink on Boxing Day, December 26th, 1983,' says
Hugo. 'I'd been feeling a bit under the weather and I just thought,
I have to do this, I can't keep going. I think I was fed up. It may be
just as simple as that.'

He stopped drinking; he stopped smoking. Joan sits in her
kitchen today surrounded by her grandchildren and says, 'I never,
ever thought he could do it. I had stopped hoping.'

That hope was entertained sparingly in the first months. When
he didn't appear to have had a drink in the next few days,
particularly at such a time of year when he was playing and the
pressure to be sociable was at its most extreme, Joan and Suzanne
were mildly surprised. So was he. They waited patiently for the
lapse.

One afternoon, Suzanne came home from school to discover that
Hugo had shaved off his moustache, and when he asked her what
she thought about it, she broke down in tears. He was at a total loss
as to what had upset her, until he realised that she thought he must

have been back on the drink and had taken the head-staggers with the razor. When he recounts this story, as he has many times to many people, he still appears stunned, even horrified, that his behaviour had led his own daughter to regard him in that way.

Joan would also search the most casual everyday incidents for indications that he'd taken a drink:

> He was out one time and there was this ringing on the
> doorbell. When I went to answer it, it was him. He said
> he'd forgotten his keys and I thought, right, he's been
> out drinking and lost them somewhere. But he hadn't.
> All he'd done was forget his keys.

She had become so accustomed to nothing being normal in his life that an ordinary moment of forgetfulness seemed unbelievable.

Suzanne turned fourteen, and as 1984 progressed it seemed that Hugo was standing by his decision. Although his star in the music business had fallen low, he was still playing, mainly in licensed premises and large summer events, where there was drink in abundance. By the time he got to Christmas 1984, he'd been one year off the drink. If ever there was a time when he would yield to temptation, this was it, and some sense of the living from day to day that all three of the family shared can be gleaned from what happened on Christmas Eve.

That day Hugo was out playing and meeting friends in a local pub. One part of his behaviour that had changed almost immediately when he stopped drinking was that he came home when he said he would. On this day he didn't. As the time slipped by, mother and daughter came to the same conclusion – he'd been waylaid by some old drinking cronies. When he eventually arrived home, their fears appeared justified. 'He was stinking of cigarette smoke,' Joan recalls, 'and he'd always smoked when he drank, and there was the smell of the pub and drink.' But there was also something strange. His eyes were clear, he didn't slur, and he wasn't wobbling. He had been in the pub, which was packed and smoky, and he'd then given some of his friends lifts home, which explained why he was late. He hadn't taken any drink at all and it was only then that Joan and Suzanne could allow themselves to think that maybe this Christmas present was going to last for a while after all.

Hugo's years of drinking were closely associated with his music career, yet when he gave up the drink, singing was the only thing he had to turn to. He had no money, he had no gear, no van; various bands had come and gone and the supporting cushion of owners and managers had disappeared. Not because they didn't like him; he'd simply become too much trouble to bother with. When it came to trying to pick up the pieces at the start of 1984, there were people prepared to give him a second chance, because although he'd been a pain, an unreliable pain at times, he'd never done anyone more harm than he'd done himself. If they'd washed their hands of him, it was out of frustration, not because they didn't think he could do the job any more; he could, if he gave himself a chance.

Hugo was enormously fortunate to enlist the help and support of Willie John Carlin and Bernard Donaghy as he tried to rebuild his life and his career. Like himself, Willie John had been born and reared in the Head of the Town, and like himself, Willie John had spent much of his life in a contest with drink, most of the time spent on the losing side. He was an older man, a neighbour of the family, and he'd known Susie well. He was regarded as a clever man who was well read and had published a book about the history of the railway in Strabane. He had also kicked his addiction to alcohol and, for this fact alone, he was held in high regard and respect by the community. 'Willie John was one of the few people who really knew what I was going through,' says Hugo.

For years, Hugo had paid little attention to the practicalities of living; he had no need to when he was entertaining the party with his drinking money. He ignored legal requirements, such as paying tax, and he kept no record of his earnings or outgoings. Willie John and Bernard knew about these matters; what's more, they knew the correct people to talk to and, most importantly, their word was respected by those with whom they dealt. A redoubtable local councillor, Willie John recounted such a sad story for the dole man that, although the latter had a reputation for sticking to the rules, he tore up Hugo's papers with a tear in his eye and let him start again. 'What Willie John was doing was helping me get a clean sheet,' says Hugo, 'because he knew that it was easy to get dragged back in.'

It was Willie John who introduced Hugo to Bernard. 'Accountant' was what it said on his door but, like Willie, Bernard did much more than that. He helped to sort out those problems that got people into difficulty in the first place and, like Willie, he became a friend to Hugo. Bernard showed Hugo how to budget for the outgoings of running his own affairs, paying musicians, hiring a van and so on, and helped him to keep track of the money as his singing career started to pick up once again.

He also had friends who had simply never given up on him. His neighbour from Innisfree Gardens, Gerard Hughes, better known as Stim, was one who lectured Hugo about his drinking but, at the same time, didn't dismiss him as beyond help. It's not surprising that these friendships continue today, for such people helped Hugo to manage his drink problem.

But now that he had caught himself on, he needed the practical support and experience of others to stay on that road and in the music business too there were enough of his old acquaintances who were prepared to help Hugo get back on his feet. There was Mickey Christie, who'd played at his wedding and his mother's funeral, an older man and a good family friend who'd played in bands all his life. And Pio McCann, long-time travelling companion, room-mate and drinking buddy. There were friends like Paddy Bradley and John Campbell, who had the contacts and experience to start getting gigs sorted out for Hugo and never seemed to mind giving of their time.

Between the four of them they also managed to sort Hugo out with equipment and even tracked down a spare van for him to use, for Hugo had nothing.

During 1984, he gradually put together another band with local musicians such as Sam Connelly, Eugene McColgan and Tom Gray, men he has now known for half a lifetime, and while it may seem that he was incredibly lucky that so many were prepared to help him relaunch his career and his life, Hugo certainly believes there was more to it than luck: 'I have never had any doubt in my mind that Wee Susie continues to pray for me, and no time did she do that more than when Joan and I were picking up the pieces in 1984.'

Paddy and John approached Jim Gough and Billy McBurney of Homespun Records about the possibility of getting Hugo back into the recording studio, and they agreed to help. Their main recording engineer, Cel Fey, was a man of very dry wit who encouraged Hugo through insults rather than praise – something he remembers with fondness:

> Cel was what we would call these days, cool. He used to sit beside these two big reel-to-reel tape recorders called Studers. The tape on them was about three inches wide and he had them all linked up and synchronised so he wouldn't have to move off his seat to do anything. He smoked all the time and he took great pride in being able to get to the end of a cigarette without any of the ash having fallen off. A great sound engineer all the same.

Going back to his roots and those who knew him best struck gold. Even the local name seemed to augur well, because Billy McBurney's decision to release 'Brady of Strabane' well and truly placed Hugo back in the spotlight. Pio had a show on one of the pirate stations and the local singer and the local song gave him the chance to talk up his friend's revival; indeed, in his broadcasting career, Pio continues to present several shows on Highland Radio in Donegal and has always been a stalwart on-air supporter of Hugo. But 'Brady of Strabane' did not only reinforce the strong sense of local identity that is so important for Irish country artists, it also suggested a promotional angle to Billy that lifted Hugo's profile at just the most effective time.

Billy had contacts in UTV, and with his encouragement, they agreed to do a feature on Hugo in his home town, and as is ever the case with local television coverage, a large number of people, a couple of hundred thousand, saw part of the programme. This doesn't mean they liked either Hugo or the music, but with viewing audiences so high, a considerable number were surely reminded of the Wee Man from Strabane, to whom they had danced ten or fifteen years ago. Better still, for Hugo there were echoes of the early days with the Tall Men and *Reach for the Stars*, with people rolling down their car windows to shout, 'Hey Hugo! Saw you on the TV the other night! You were looking well!'

And his faithful fans still wanted him. As the diary filled out and the spread of venues continued to grow, friends and fans alike left him in no doubt that they were delighted to see him in control of his life and to hear him doing what he did best – entertaining them and enjoying it into the bargain. And while that delighted him, the fact that he could earn an income pleased him just as much. 'It wasn't just nice words people said to me,' says Hugo, 'they were prepared to pay good money to come and see the band again and they were prepared to buy the new records, so I was back to making a living out of singing.'

The money that Hugo was earning was 'real money', as he calls it. There were no cheques. Hugo was paid out of the notes that were taken at the door, usually in accordance with what was agreed before the gig, but not always. One night a promoter remarked that he didn't think Hugo and his band had performed as well as he had expected and maybe he should keep something back. Hugo left the office and returned a few minutes later with the poster that had advertised the night's event. He laid it out on the desk and pointed out that it stated 'Hugo Duncan, The Wee Man From Strabane, Dancing 10.00 until 1.00', which was exactly what had happened. It made no reference to whether they might play very well or only reasonably well. He got his money.

Hugo would pay the band what was owed and take the rest of the cash home. It came in all denominations, large and small. Hugo would store up the returns from several nights and then sit down at the kitchen table for the sheer pleasure of counting it. 'You could have three, four, five hundred pounds, all different colours, all mixed up, and all the wrong way round. And I'd sort it all out into its different piles and then add the whole lot up,' Hugo says with a grin.

Arguably, it was the first time he'd made anything approaching a living out of singing, for, this time, the money was managed and not scattered to the four corners of the nearest lounge bar – Bernard Donaghy saw to that. A measure of how swiftly his popularity and earning power grew once he adopted a more normal, productive lifestyle is that in 1985 Hugo and Joan moved into the first house they'd owned since they got married fifteen years earlier, which is quite a while to wait to be carried over the threshold. With the weight he'd put on, she could scarcely lift him.

Help and support also came from unexpected quarters. A man called John Brannigan, who has since become a friend of Hugo's, got talking to him at a barn dance in Newcastle, County Down. They didn't know each other from Adam. John said he enjoyed the music but that Hugo wasn't doing himself any favours by using an antique sound system and that he either needed to get himself a sound engineer who could work miracles or some decent PA equipment. Hugo shrugged his shoulders, rolled his eyes and pointed out a few of the financial truths about how much it cost to get a show on the road, from scratch:

We chatted away and then I went back on stage. About
a fortnight later, I met him again and he said he had
something for me and he handed me an envelope with
enough money in it to buy the PA system that we
needed. He just gave it to me, there and then, and
when I asked him why he was being so generous, he
said I'd played at his wife's twenty-first birthday and it
was one of the best nights of her life.

Gradually Hugo got back to playing six nights a week during the
summer, and though the audiences were never as big as they'd been
in the last days of the showbands, he could easily turn four, five and
six hundred. So there was plenty for Bernard to keep him advised
on, but not even he could prevent Hugo's past sins and his
revitalised profile from conspiring to scupper him.

By the mid-eighties, Hugo had a couple of albums on release, one
with Billy's Homespun label, another with Tony Loughman's Top
Spin label. 'Come Down from the Mountain, Katie Daly' and 'Brady
of Strabane' were doing very well for him, so his recordings were
advertised on television. This didn't escape the notice of one of the
banks that had lent him money to buy yet another car while he was
still on the drink. It sounds a bit like the plot outline for a sitcom, to
lend money to a man who had none because he drank it all in order
to buy a car that he would drive when he was drunk. No matter;
what annoyed the bank was that, in ten years no money had been
paid against the loan and the debt still stood at several hundred
pounds. Now, to make matters worse, the manager couldn't have his
tea in peace without seeing the debtor on television crooning, 'If We
Only had Old Ireland Over Here'. He promptly decided to get Old
Duncan over here and into the small claims court.

Hugo attended the hearing in his oldest, most well-worn clothes.
The magistrate observed that his records were advertised on

television, and surely that meant he was successful? No, Hugo replied, the advertising was paid for by the record company in an effort to try and make him successful. He had a new car, she noticed. It was on the HP, he said. How did he pay for his television? It was rented. How come he had a video player? He needed it to view his promotional material and, anyway, it too was rented. And where, she wished to know, did the money come from to pay these debts? Hugo said all the money he earned from singing had to be handed over to an accountant, who made sure that his current creditors were dealt with and that money was set aside for the running of the house.

All of this was more or less true, his money was managed on his behalf, but the matter that sealed the case in his favour was when he made the point that being advertised on television didn't mean he had money; it meant that someone else had money.

The magistrate ruled that Mr Duncan was not to be pursued any further for his old debt.

Money is important to Hugo and it's one of the drives that keeps him working so hard, but equally important is his love of performance. Each time he finishes a live show, Hugo wants to do another and he won't consider giving up until the fun goes out of it; that will be the day to stop. 'Even in the bad days, unless I was very drunk, singing was the only time I felt half normal,' he says. 'Today I still love it. There are three places I'm happiest: at home with the grandchildren, in the radio studio, and on stage singing.'

It's over twenty-five years since Hugo's friends helped sort him out and Hugo repays the debt by doing the same for others. He will listen to their problems, particularly if they're drink-related, and if he can give some advice, he will; if not, he will just listen, for he knows what it meant when he needed someone to listen to him. He has one rule only: 'If someone comes to me in drink, I say, come back when you're sober and we'll tackle it then.'

When first asked if he would address pupils at schools about the dangers of drinking, he was uneasy about what he could say to young teenagers and far from certain that he could make any connection with them at all. But the first thing the pupils realised was that he was talking for real – this was not a teacher talking about a subject he had read about, it was a man talking about something that had happened to him. It was authentic. The second thing they realised was that they could talk freely to him and he answered in their language, for he was neither a teacher nor an adviser. The fact that he was a broadcaster mattered not a lot, for he was not of their generation; indeed, he was several generations removed. Then and now, he tells them the truth and knows that he makes his mark, because he can see it:

> It's in their faces. It's in the questions they ask
> afterwards. They know someone close to them, in their
> family maybe, who does what I did. Sometimes they
> won't dare ask me in front of others, but they'll come
> later and I'll listen.

The greatest support of all came from Joan and Suzanne, who gradually were able to replace doubt with confidence and have experienced better years than they had dared to hope for back in 1983. They both understand that they have a different problem to deal with today: Hugo's constant efforts to make up for the lost years. He tries to replace what has gone with material things: he gives presents. Joan can take as many trips to Lourdes as she wishes, take her sister if she wants. Even though Suzanne is happily settled with her own family, he constantly asks her if she's all right for money. He can't buy back that time but he'll keep trying, because it's probably the only gesture he can make.

Joan is a person of few words in public but she has said that, as the realisation dawned that the nightmare was over, it seemed to her that her world became 'so light and airy'. She's also quick to point out that Hugo has not withdrawn himself from social life, and she's surprised how easy he is in the presence of drink:

> He'll go down to Christie's on Christmas Day and sing
> with people drinking all around him. If someone calls
> to the house over the holiday, he'll offer a drink at ten
> o'clock in the morning. Sometimes I don't know how
> he does it.

But once a reputation is established, it can take a long time to shift. Some years later, when Hugo and the film critic Barry Norman were guests on the *Gerry Kelly Show*, Hugo was chatting about his years of drinking. Barry was fascinated by the story and asked him if he could ever see himself taking a drink again. Hugo said there was an outside possibility he might have one on the day of his daughter's marriage. It was another five years before Suzanne's wedding, and for the record, he didn't have a drink. The day after the wedding, however, a man stopped him on the street in Strabane and said that he'd had a drink in two or three bars in the town the night before, and in each the question had arisen at some point of the conversation: 'Well, I wonder did Drunken Duncan go back on the drink at the wedding?' Long runs the fox.

Hugo has never sought to blame his drinking years on any aspect of his upbringing, least of all on the early death of Wee Susie. On that suggestion he is adamant:

> If there was any blessing to my mother dying so young,
> it was that she never knew me when I had the drink on
> me. I always regret that she never saw me when I was
> successful, never knew that I was on TV, played halls
> with two thousand, three thousand people and that I
> have my own radio show. But if she'd known about the
> drink and the hurt, she would also have seen me at my
> worst and that would have broken her heart.

Slimmed down to catch the girls

Hugo and Joan's wedding day, 2 April 1970

With Joan's sister Margaret and niece Yolanda

With bridesmaid Margaret and best man John Sharkey

With Suzanne

A busy schedule for a rising star, Christmas 1972

Just one of the many bands that Hugo fronted

Hugo on stage at the Grand Opera House –
or the Grand Ole Opry as Hugo prefers to call it
COURTESY OF PACEMAKER PRESS INTERNATIONAL

Hugo with Philomena Begley and Brian Coll,
after the filming of a *Hugo and Friends* show
COURTESY OF PACEMAKER PRESS INTERNATIONAL

Tom T. Hall and Hugo, outside Tom's house in Nashville

Hugo with one of his heroes, Charley Pride
COURTESY OF BBC NORTHERN IRELAND

Hugo at one of the many outside broadcasts he presents each year. Joanne Murphy (aka The Wee Woman with the Big Stick) is in front of the stage with headphones on.

Hard at work in the studio

9

Turn Your Radio On

When I was on the bottle, I never knew how much of my time was spent doing nothing. When I got used to waking early in the morning with a clear head and knowing that the rest of the day was mine to either waste or do something with, it was scary at first. But I had wasted enough of those days.

It is possible that if Hugo had never taken to drink, he would not have become a broadcaster. When he gave up the drink, much of his life was in a mess and in his efforts to sort it out he unintentionally created a second chance to consider propositions and ambitions, some of which had never occurred to him before. In an ironic way, the drink gave him back himself. As the first sober days became sober weeks and then sober months, his rediscovered ability to think clearly and objectively helped him appreciate what had really been happening in his life. And with that came the realisation that though he'd made a bit of a hames of things, he could also put them right.

Since 1983 Hugo has always risen early, this despite the fact that he frequently doesn't go to bed till the small hours, and until he started working at the BBC's Ormeau Avenue headquarters in Belfast in 1998, he was a daily attender at Mass. His body clock is permanently locked in gig time, so even if he's not on the road, he whiles away the evening with the satellite channels, or these days, surfing the net. He is rarely still; there is always some matter to attend to. Long before a sizeable chunk of the day was spent travelling to and from Belfast for his radio and television work, he had taken control of his own affairs in the music business: handling contracts, promotion, musicians, recordings, and CD, video and DVD releases. Before that, he used the hours in the day to get himself back on the straight and narrow.

There is a sense that he is making up for what cannot be retrieved. For twenty-five years he has pushed himself to keep the diary filled; he travels as far for work today as he did when he was twenty and his eye is ever open for the next opportunity. He knows that luck and Susie's prayers played a hand in his renewal, and he's a firm believer that that's often enough to help swing the balance. 'What I needed was for some things to go my way,' he says. 'I had my family; there were good people who helped me; and then small things happened that would give me a lift.'

In 1985 he was presented with a gold disc in recognition of his record sales over the years. The impact of this was twofold.

Like any performer worth his salt, Hugo is forever in search of attention. To go on stage, sit in front of a microphone or peer into a television camera, especially as the front man, requires a special sort of determination, some would say arrogance. It certainly requires a great deal of faith in one's ability to perform and most ordinary mortals will confess they can think of nothing worse than having to speak in front of others and be the centre of attention. And being at the centre means that some of those watching are as content to see trial and tribulation as to see success. A glance at the showbiz pages of any newspaper or magazine will provide ample evidence of this.

To be a performer, therefore, demands a certain character, not least because it's a very vulnerable role and that's why performers are always seeking evidence that what they're doing is good, that people enjoy it, that they matter to us. Hugo's producer, the Wee Woman with the Big Stick, for example, laments that unless she reminds him at least ten times a day that he's the best product the BBC has and that his listeners adore him, he can be an absolute torture to work with. He has even been known to sulk. It's hard to believe his sixtieth birthday will roll around soon.

So the gold disc acted as a bit of therapy.

It also served to remind others that Hugo was still around; pirate radio station owners, for instance. In 1985 such stations were unlicensed, so instead of paying for the frequencies on which they broadcast, they simply stole them by setting up a small transmitter and worked away on that frequency until someone with a rule book tracked them down. To be fair to the pirate radio operators, buying a licence was practically impossible because the regulation regarding radio transmission was totally influenced by the major public service and commercial broadcasters, which usually didn't target small communities or areas of the country with low-density population.

There were major pirate radio names like Caroline and Kiss, but in Ireland, most stations outside Dublin were broadcasting to small communities and, indeed, frequently included the word 'community' in their station idents. Pirate radio was a hugely popular form of entertainment in the mid-eighties and stations based in border areas boasted a peculiar advantage, for they were based where police, north and south, were understandably less likely to mount lightning raids in search of transmitter gear.

Hugo made several appearances on pirate radio to talk about his gold disc and this included visits to two of the stations closest to home, North West Community Radio (NWCR) in Buncrana and Donegal Community Radio (DCR) in Letterkenny. Bobby McDaid owned DCR and the day after the award was presented, he asked Hugo if he fancied presenting a show on the station. The suggestion was not, would he like to go away and think about the proposal? It was, would he like to present a show – that afternoon? Of course he would, and he did.

Becoming a broadcaster had never crossed Hugo's mind, and though he hadn't a clue whether he would be any good, the notion appealed to him, and to his ego. Bobby's casual invitation set in train a course of events that ultimately led Hugo to his own television series for the BBC, his daily radio show for BBC Radio Ulster, and radio and television programmes from the town that any Irish country star has on his list of Ten Places To Go Before I Die – Nashville.

None of this would have happened if Hugo hadn't taken up Bobby's offer. In those days, BBC radio programmes were hosted by presenters who were skilled in the art of broadcasting. If they presented music programmes, it was usually the case that they were broadcasters who had an interest in certain genres. Hence, Walter Love was a newsreader with a love of jazz; Paddy O'Flaherty was a reporter with a love of American country music. The pirate stations tended to schedule presenters more for their local knowledge than their on-air skills. It saved having to have a pronunciation unit.

So Hugo's first radio home was a pirate station. To be honest, he wasn't very good, and that comes from no higher authority than Hugo himself. But whatever his standard in the early days, he was popular with the listeners and the owners and he continued to broadcast regularly on DCR and NWCR until the pirate stations were closed down by the authorities in December 1988.

But not before Hugo had discovered that he enjoyed talking about the music he loves and that he derived great pleasure from sharing the music with others. Country and Irish music is ingrained in the border counties of Donegal, Derry, Leitrim, Cavan, Fermanagh, Tyrone and Louth and he personally knew the artists that were played on air. He knew the songs – he sang the songs. He recognised the addresses on cards and letters asking for requests and dedications; as he read through them, he realised he knew the people who had sent them in. His broadcasting style was hesitant, punctuated by much umming and aahing, and the chat was limited, but he didn't sound out of place to listeners who judged a radio station by the number of local and personal name checks it broadcast rather than the slickness or supposed professionalism of its presentation. These listeners wanted advertisements that mentioned local shops, lists of events and what's-ons that had nothing to do with the urban centres of Derry, Dublin or Belfast, and songs sung by artists they could see playing somewhere near their homes. Not only did Hugo not sound out of place, he didn't feel out of place. He enjoyed it:

> Here was something that interested me. I don't sit
> down and read books; I stopped going to the pictures
> after I was engaged; when I watch TV, I just flick. All I
> know is music, my music, and as well as singing it for
> people, I now found that I could talk to them about it
> and they would be interested.

Radio also introduced him to the thrill of total strangers coming up to him in the street or at a show and saying, 'I heard you on the radio the other day, Hugo.' He loved it.

His journey from the bottle to the *Radio Times* was under way, but he was championing music that was more and more frequently described as 'hick from the sticks'.

Since Hugo had taken up the reins as a professional singer and entertainer in 1970, enormous changes had taken place in Irish culture. The blues and rock business had found a natural home in Ireland, in particular in the cities of Belfast, Dublin and, to a lesser extent, Cork. By the time that Hugo made his debut on pirate radio, Van Morrison had long since left Sammy Houston's Jazz Club and the Maritime in Belfast. Having introduced a new generation to traditional music as it was never played in their parents' day, Horslips had more or less been and gone. In the year that Hugo got himself seriously involved with the drink, Thin Lizzy stood at Number One in the Irish charts with 'Whiskey in the Jar', and by the time that Hugo began his broadcasting career in 1986, Rory Gallagher's new year concerts in Belfast's Ulster Hall had become the stuff of legend.

However, the continuing surprise about Ireland is that despite its enormous contribution to the worlds of rock and pop, there is a long and enduring folk memory and, in varying degrees, many people continue to be fans of folk and traditional music. They are fans not in any specialist sense and a purist might wince at the music they enjoy, but there is still a fondness for songs like 'The Town I Love so Well', 'A Mother's Love's a Blessing', 'The Hills of Donegal', 'Carrickfergus', and so on. The set list of 1968 can easily be the set list of 2008, whether others consider it hick or not.

By the time the pirate radio stations were closed down, Hugo had been back on the music road, sober, for nearly five years and had friends who were happy to support him, like Pat Derry, who broadcast from the BBC's station in the North-West, Radio Foyle. Hugo was a frequent visitor to the station, which prided itself on maintaining an open-door policy despite the years of trouble in the city. This gave Radio Foyle a feel and an atmosphere that was closer to the community radio of its hinterland than the classic BBC style found in Belfast. So it suited Hugo rightly and he got to know the folk who worked there and, in turn, they became well used to him.

Hugo was asked to fill in for a couple of weeks on Don O'Doherty's daily radio show. Don was a well-known and popular figure in Derry who'd been on the airwaves since Radio Foyle opened and who was renowned for his charitable works in the city. Nevertheless, there was a feeling in the BBC that it was time for a change, so they were looking around for possible replacements. Whether or not Hugo was a serious contender is a moot point, given the presence of other more experienced presenters who hailed from the city, but there was a slight concern that the local press might get a whiff of change in the air, no matter who would replace Don. So in order to keep matters quiet, yet allow Hugo the time to learn how to operate the technical equipment and rehearse the format of the show, he was smuggled in at night when no one was around to ask why he was being trained up as a presenter. To what extent he was even regarded as a presenter is debatable; he was recognised more for his celebrity status with the country music audience.

Hugo's first producer at Radio Foyle was himself very new to the job but no stranger to the world of celebrity. Mickey Bradley was bass player with the Undertones, whose anthem to eternal youth, 'Teenage Kicks', is just as far removed from 'Dear God' or 'My Donegal Rose' as one could possibly imagine. With this in mind, Mickey decided to set their musical tastes aside and concentrate on getting Hugo into shape. 'Mickey was very clear on what he wanted,' Hugo recalls. 'The first night he says to me, "Just you remember you're not here because you're a broadcaster, you're here because you're Hugo Duncan, no other reason." Talk about getting put in your place.'

And so it was announced that Don O'Doherty was taking leave and Hugo would replace him for a few weeks. Don came back from leave, resumed his old seat and lost his programme shortly afterwards. Hugo has felt ever since that Don blamed him for prising him out of his slot, but nothing could be further from the truth, not least because it wasn't Hugo Duncan that got the job, it was Sean Coyle. Hugo had simply been a convenient distraction. As far as listeners were concerned, he was known and probably liked, but no one would have imagined that he would replace Don on a full-time basis, so no one went sniffing to see what was going on; until it happened. And by then Don was gone.

But Hugo wasn't. He was still very much there. He was offered a programme on Friday afternoons between four and five, and soon afterwards, he was given a similar slot on Mondays. He suited the BBC because he was from the broadcasting patch of Radio Foyle but not from the city itself, and the perception of the station's output depended very much on which side of the river its listeners lived. Hugo was different; he had nothing to do with the city. He came from Strabane, a place about which most Derry residents on both river banks would share a view, not always complimentary. He was also into country music, which was entirely acceptable to all sides of the equation.

There was one other factor that stood him in good stead – Hugo was no trouble. He didn't come with the attitude that he was somehow superior and that he should be recognised as such. He didn't make demands or argue with his bosses, nor did he assume that, because he held down one bit of broadcasting territory, he was an expert on all aspects of the BBC. In short, he was not a pain and could be left to get on with the job quite happily once he'd been taught the ropes. Such presenters are a godsend to stations like Radio Foyle, which have limited resources and whose management has neither the staff nor the time to engage in constant massaging. He did what he was asked and he was a bit of crack.

Some time later, a new station manager, Charlie Warmington, was tasked with extending Foyle's hours of output into the weekend. This is always a mixed blessing for any manager or producer. On the one hand, it offers more output and a chance for the station to increase its profile; on the other hand, finding people who are happy to give up part of their weekends can be a challenge.

At the end of the eighties, Saturday afternoons were for sport, shopping and DIY. There was none of the staggered sports coverage that exists today, with matches from Saturday lunchtime through to late Sunday afternoon. So Charlie, who didn't have the resources to mount a big sports programme, decided that fans of country music might be the very ones who would be prepared to tune in on a Saturday afternoon if they had a show targeted directly at them. Hugo was the obvious choice but his weekends were filled up, not with sport, but with music, travelling to gigs across the north of Ireland. What was needed was a carrot.

Charlie suggested that the one programme the Radio Ulster schedule was crying out for was an Irish country music show, a show in which the content was as likely to be delivered by Irish singers as their more famous and more frequently played counterparts from Nashville and beyond. If Saturday afternoons were considered something of a desert on radio, early Saturday nights were even worse, but it was this slot that Charlie proposed. After all, if the idea didn't work, there wasn't a large audience to lose anyway.

So Hugo was offered his own country music show on Radio Foyle on Saturday afternoons and a further country music show on Radio Ulster on Saturday evenings. Hugo, always the businessman, saw immediately what Charlie had meant him to see: if his Saturday night gig was in the west of the country, he could present both programmes from the studios in Radio Foyle; if his gig was in the east of the country, he could present both shows from the studios in Belfast. If the gig was in the middle of the country, he could toss a coin.

Hugo was now reaping the benefit of being no trouble, with a reputation for getting on with the job in hand. He didn't need anyone to look after him. No one knew the local country scene better than he, so as long as he had a few people to take the phone calls, Hugo was self-sufficient.

The listeners liked him. They wrote in for requests; they sent in details of events they were attending over the weekend; they phoned up with dedications; they took part in the simple competitions; and when they let him know they were listening with the children, he gave himself the nickname Uncle Hugo.

In turn, Hugo relayed all his listeners' requests and information with gusto, coupled with many demands to be kept informed as to how things were going. He was like a talking version of the combined Social, Personal and Events columns of a parochial newspaper and every bit as closely followed by those who knew what was on offer.

He was rehearsing an early blueprint for his future daily slot, *Country Afternoon*.

Things tend to happen slowly in the world of radio, and so it was in Hugo's case. Changes in schedule can take a long time to bed down. Once in place, it will often be a long time before change is considered again. New programmes have to build their audiences and programmes that are on only once a week can run for many years before they are truly felt to have found their place. So Hugo gradually became part of the broadcasting furniture of BBC radio in Northern Ireland. In an operation primarily based in Belfast, he represented a community situated on the other side of the country. He also represented a culture that found little empathy within Broadcasting House on Ormeau Avenue, so other than those in management that placed the programmes in the schedule and helped look after them, there wasn't much attention paid to Hugo's shows.

In a way, this suited him, for he was able to practise on air. He could make mistakes and learn from them without anyone panicking that the whole station might collapse round them. Most importantly, he talked to and listened to an audience which felt that its tastes and culture had not been well catered for by the BBC. By going his own sweet way over all those Saturday afternoons and nights that stretched into years, he was discovering a community that wanted to be in touch with itself and hear what its members were up to.

Hugo had always been popular with listeners on Radio Foyle, but that was probably to be expected. On Radio Ulster, his evening show began to return good listening figures and the volumes of written mail and telephone calls received were impressive. He was fun to have around and any member of BBC management visiting Foyle would find that Hugo was always there to be bumped into, accidentally. It became a matter of course that within several weeks of the VIP's visit, Hugo's latest CD or music video would find its way onto that manager's desk with a note reminding him or her that he was a star in the making and not to forget that 'Your Uncle Hugo loves you'.

In 1998, BBC Radio Ulster was performing very strongly. It outdid all its rivals and the numbers listening across the day were very high;

a strand such as Talkback could attract 150,000 listeners, close to a tenth of the population and a figure that many television programme-makers would be pleased to get. The reputation of most radio stations is staked on the business they do during the day, Monday to Friday, so strong figures between 7 a.m. and 6 p.m. usually mean a good performance.

However, this pattern is not uniform throughout the day. The heaviest listening time for radio is in the mornings. By twelve o'clock, people have started to switch to daytime television, and in 1998 soaps like *Neighbours* and *Home and Away* signalled a big television switch-on at half past one. People also go off to have lunch and then begin afternoon activities, such as shopping, collecting children, housework. Radio Ulster fitted this pattern with one exception. The presence of Talkback had delayed the switch-off on radio from twelve o'clock until one o'clock. Radio Ulster listeners stayed with the station until the news headlines at one o'clock and then they left.

The question that came up for discussion was, if listeners could be persuaded once to break the average listening pattern, could they be persuaded to do it again? Who out there would want to listen to a programme so much that they would be happy to give up *Columbo*, the afternoon racing, and quiz shows, not to mention collecting the children and doing their work.

Anna Carragher, head of broadcast, and Pat Loughrey, the controller of the BBC in Northern Ireland, wondered if the Irish country music audience, which at that time was regarded as mainly rural, might want a programme of its own. The thinking was sound. Critics of BBC services pointed to the fact that not only was the radio and television output managed from Belfast, most of it was made there too, so it couldn't possibly reflect the interests of those who lived in Fermanagh and Tyrone, north Antrim or Armagh. Just as with Charlie Warmington's Saturday evening gamble, the argument went that they could afford to take a chance because there wasn't that much of an audience to lose, and they began to think that Hugo might be their man.

There were two possible hitches. Hugo lived in Strabane and did most of his broadcasting from Foyle. There already was a Radio Ulster daily programme based in Foyle, Gerry Anderson's show, and much and all as there was a desire to represent all six counties, it was felt that it might be a step too far to have two daily strands coming from outside Belfast. Hugo would have to come to Radio Ulster and nobody knew whether he would or not. The other hitch was that Irish country music was not embraced with enthusiasm by production staff in BBC Belfast and there were many influential figures outside the BBC who failed to see anything cultural in it at all. It could be tolerated when it was on Radio Foyle or late in the evening on Radio Ulster, but never in the daytime. The two hitches together meant that someone had to find out if Hugo could be enticed to Belfast, without giving him any commitment or raising the slightest possibility that word might get out. Hugo remembers when he was first approached with the idea:

> I got this phone call from Paul Evans who was head of production. He said to me, 'This call never happened but if you were asked to present a daily show from Belfast, would that be a problem? This is only a question; it's not a suggestion. You might never get asked, so it might never be an issue.' I didn't know what he was on about. All I knew was that someone was suggesting something I had dreamed of but never, ever expected to happen. Go to Belfast? I'd have gone to the moon.

Hugo presented his first afternoon show from Studio 8 on the fifth floor of the BBC building in Belfast at half past one on 5 October 1998, and he's still there.

10

Don't Give Up the Night Job

If Hugo could have dreamed up his ideal job, it's doubtful if he could have bettered what had actually happened to him when he joined Radio Ulster. He loves entertaining, enjoys a bit of banter and crack, and adores country music; here he was being paid to do just that. If there was any drawback, it might have been the travelling. Having agreed that he would present the new programme from Belfast, Hugo was now faced with the return trip from Strabane to Belfast five days a week, one hundred and eighty miles a day, not counting diversions. It meant that at least three hours of each day would be spent driving. But he wasn't about to let that get in the way. He was used to travelling the length and breadth of the country, and up until now, many of the miles had been covered in the evening, on the way to a gig, or in the wee small hours of the morning, on the way home. That didn't worry him, for he never went to bed early anyhow. Determined to keep all avenues open, he also continued his work at Radio Foyle. As a result, he was faced with the prospect of occasionally broadcasting seven days a week.

All Hugo's broadcasting was live and one of his early fears was the possibility of something going wrong at any moment. He might play the wrong music; he might turn a knob and blast the ears off his listeners; perhaps worse, he might turn a knob and there would be silence and he wouldn't have a notion as to why. Those who are now used to his relaxed flow of banter probably do not realise that one of his greatest fears was running out of things to say. At the start he found that the easy bit was saying, 'Brian Coll there for Angela and her husband in Doagh'; the hard part was deciding what to say next.

Although Hugo hoped that some of his listeners already knew him from his Radio Ulster and Radio Foyle weekend programmes, in those first months he had no real sense of who the audience was on weekday afternoons. He didn't know what these people were doing as they listened to his new show, whether they were working, driving, listening at home, on their own or with the children; so rather than feel that he was speaking to an empty space, he focused his delivery on the studio clock.

In his direct line of sight as he sat at the controls on the studio desk was one of the many clocks, set to the precise second, that rule the beginnings and ends of programmes. Hugo developed the habit, which continues to this day, of reading requests and dedications and delivering his bits and pieces of chat to the clock. For him, it represents the ear of the listener and he concentrates on it rather than just talking to thin air.

So, in addition to the nervous energy that accompanies any live broadcast, Hugo was also dealing with the pressure of whether he could cope and whether the listeners would stay with him or desert him.

He also had to consider the question of what the BBC would make of his performance, for he knew that only continued support from those who had the faith to give him this opportunity, coupled with a positive response from the listeners, would be enough to fend off those who did not like this change of strategy in the afternoon schedule. This was a slot that had previously been occupied at various times by social action programmes, documentaries, specially commissioned studio sessions featuring the cream of Northern Ireland's musicians, and experienced music broadcasters with strong reputations; none of which had ever pulled in decent audiences.

Hugo was embarking on an anxious and exhausting time, on top of which he was committed to performing three or four gigs a week, which meant even more mileage and more of his energy. After a day's work in Belfast, there could have been the temptation to put on his slippers at night and doze by the fire; but then, that had never been the Duncan style. Having weighed everything up, Hugo ignored the slippers and decided to keep on the road and continue with his playing career – even though his new job demanded a pretty hefty working week – and he did so for three principal reasons.

In his own mind, he was convinced that the afternoon show on Radio Ulster would be short-lived. At the outset, no one could predict how the audience would respond; those who analysed the figures and statistics knew that Hugo had a distinct and loyal following, but whether that following would seek him out at lunchtime was anybody's guess. His first contract was issued for six months and that confirmed his worry that this was very much a trial run that could be pulled at any moment. The truth is that the BBC had more faith in him than that, but as far as he was concerned, staying on the road gave Hugo a safety net if things didn't work out in broadcasting.

He was also thinking with the head. He knew that the BBC in Belfast had a concern that it was perceived to be associated too much with the Greater Belfast area and he understood that his new employers saw it as an asset that he was out and about engaging in person with the audience across the country on three or four nights of the week. He was a perfect fit. Here was a presenter who didn't have to be persuaded to go and meet his audience; they were already coming out in their droves to hear him. Here was a presenter who understood clearly what his audience expected, because for years he'd been discovering first hand what they liked and disliked. Here also was a presenter who knew better than those who contracted him what the music policy of his programme should be; after all, he'd been perfecting the set list since he was fifteen.

Hugo realised that the broadcasts and the live shows fed off each other. At the very least, he would return from a gig with a bundle of requests and name checks for his next radio programme. And crucially, through meeting and chatting, he was up to date with what music that night's audience was listening to and who else was due to play that venue. He was more clued in than his employers could hope to be. He was their ear to the ground with the country music audiences.

As long as he didn't advertise blatantly where his next list of gigs would take him, it was acceptable that he drop enough clues to leave those with the interest in no doubt as to where they could catch up with him. He'd become good at it. He never would say, 'I'll be performing at the Millbrook Lodge in Ballynahinch this Friday night' – too obvious. Much more likely you'd hear, 'This one's for Davy the Digger down there in Ballynahinch from his wife, Linda. You may get your dancing shoes on you, Davy boy, for I'll see you this Friday, God willing.'

The third reason for continuing to take the bookings was that performance was his life. By the time he joined the BBC, he'd been singing professionally for twenty-seven years.

From the time that he'd played Buttons in the pantomime in Saint Pat's Hall, he knew that he got a kick out of the audience's response to him. It didn't matter if the gig was a marquee packed with a thousand people dancing on wooden duckboards at a summer carnival in Cavan, or topping the bill at a Saint Patrick's Day entertainment in the Royal Albert Hall, Hugo loved the buzz. So he was excited and apprehensive about his new radio show, but he knew also that if it didn't work out he would still be doing the job he loved most – singing for the punters. And that would keep him going, give him something to do, something to believe in, just as it had done in 1983.

He's been on the road now for forty years and still does three or four dates a week. Today these will include a weekend flight to Manchester and a chauffeur-driven car to whisk him up the motorway to top the bill for six hundred English country fans in Blackpool. A couple of times a year he's flown to Tenerife and Malaga, where he's the star attraction for upwards of five hundred holidaymakers. Though he only plays for two nights on each visit, there's a free villa thrown in for a week, but he has never taken up the offer, for that would mean he'd have to relax and do nothing for a few days, which is one thing he doesn't do well. Besides, he's uncomfortable when he's away from his normal places of business; he feels out of control. As soon as the engagements are over, he flies home to settle back into the radio show. He'll deny it, but he's heart scared of somebody taking over his programme while he's away and the audience suddenly discovering that they like the replacement better than him. For the same reason, several times a year he has to be chased out of the BBC building with a yard brush and banned from coming back for a week or two, in the hope that he'll take some holidays. 'What would I do with a holiday?' he says. 'Joan, she goes to Lourdes and Fatima two or three times a year, so she's happy, and as long as she's happy, so am I. She goes and prays for a miracle and then comes home, looks at me and sees that her prayers haven't been answered.'

Over the course of any year, quite a number of Hugo's personal appearances are for formal charities, or for people who have asked him for some support and suddenly discover that he's prepared to give a bit of his time. Those in the entertainment business have a long tradition of calling on each other to create an evening's crack, share the stage and raise some money or give a boost to a worthwhile cause, and Hugo is no different. One little-known fact to surprise even the faithful is that he was a regular member of a showbiz charity football team that played most weeks in the early seventies, challenging regular teams in fund-raising matches. 'It's not as bad as it seems,' he laughs. 'I played in goals, and depending on whether I was on or off the diet, there were days I didn't have to move to save the ball. All I had to do was get in the way and my waistline did the rest.'

In four decades or so, he's played as wide a variety of venues and to as mixed an assortment of audiences as anyone on the island. Even during the worst times in Northern Ireland's history over the last thirty to forty years, there were very few places he wouldn't have played; the reason being that, to him, his band and the hundreds of other bands, it was business as usual. It was possible to stick to your local patch but difficult to break even that way, because there are only so many gigs on offer in any one place. Hugo explains:

> The band business was thirty-two-county and not just for the players. Fans would crisscross the border to follow their favourites. They always did that and during the Troubles it was no different because they had to go out, otherwise they'd have sat at home and gone mad. I never said, 'Oh, I'm not playing there.'

Everywhere they went, promoters, organisers and fans were always appreciative and full of advice about the geography of the local area. It was common to play one night in a part of the country that would be perceived as belonging to one side of the community and be welcomed with open arms: 'Great to see you, Hugo, thanks for coming. Now, you know we're all right here, but you see once you go five miles down the road on your way home, just watch out, for those boys would be up to no good.' He was just as likely the next night to be playing somewhere belonging to the other side and get exactly the same advice about their neighbours down the road.

And then, whether or not Hugo got used to considering travelling Northern Ireland's roads and working during the Troubles purely in business terms, there was a time when it mattered:

> July the 31st, 1975, when the three boys from the Miami were killed. I'd known Fran O'Toole since *Reach for the Stars* from a few years before, and though we went different ways, we'd bump into each other from time to time. I always said he'd done me the great

favour by beating me and making the country sorry for me. But the killing was a bad business and for a while we were wary.

Being wary included checking under the vans for bombs before they travelled. On the longer journeys, if the driver noticed a car had been behind them for quite a while, he'd slow down to let it pass and, as it drew level, hit the brakes, just in case someone was about to take a shot at them. On occasion the police would meet bands at the border and escort them to their gigs. 'We all did these things for a while but gradually you carried on in the old way,' Hugo recalls. 'What can you do but get on with it? I can still see Fran in the studio at RTÉ, young, slim, fair-haired. He was very chatty and I remember he took time to speak to everyone. A lovely man.'

Orange halls, GAA clubs, community associations, Presbyterian church halls, parochial halls – all have hosted Hugo Duncan gigs at some time or another in his career. He particularly enjoyed playing bonfire night on the Eleventh of July for Sammy Barr in Ballymena's Flamingo Ballroom, which served the best hot dogs in the country. The easiest mistake for the band to make was to forget momentarily which particular venue it was playing at. Launching into the nationalist ballad 'Boolavogue' would have raised a few eyebrows in the Flamingo. The same song would have been much appreciated in the Fiesta in Letterkenny. Bands could be equally unfortunate with the choice of national anthem, or whether to play it or not, and to this day it's not unknown for the band to be caught between those on the organising committee who want to be more inclusive and not play any anthem and those who wish to stick to the traditional route. 'There was one night, not so long ago,' says Hugo, 'when I said to the guy, "Let us know if you want the anthem played", and he said he'd sort it out. We had packed up and gone and they still hadn't sorted it out.'

As he looks back over ten years on Radio Ulster, it turns out that keeping the night job as well as the new day job wasn't necessary after all, but he wouldn't have had it any other way. He wasn't kicked out after six months, but like any presenter, he's anxious about change. Early in 1999, the local press had quoted Anna Carragher as saying that there would be changes to the radio schedule. Hugo immediately assumed this meant him, but several days later she stopped him in the corridor and asked him if he was looking forward to hosting his first outside broadcasts in the coming summer, so it was clear he wasn't being put out just yet. 'That's the way you found out about things,' says Hugo. 'You never went to a meeting, you just bumped into somebody, and that was your next six months sorted out. It's good to see that Joan's prayers at Lourdes worked in the end.'

But Joan's prayers nearly failed him that year, when, as a direct result of his new fame, his past crept up on him again.

It was around the month of July and Hugo's radio show had been on air for about nine months. His television work was going well and in many ways he was flavour of the moment. The phone in the car rang; it was Suzy O'Hara, assistant to the controller of the BBC in Northern Ireland. This immediately worried Hugo, for his first assumption when anyone in a position of authority is looking for him is that he's done something wrong, but as he listened initially, for once, he thought he might be mistaken.

'Hiya, Hugo. It's Suzy here. I have some good news.'

'That's great, Suzy.'

'And some bad news.'

'Oh, that's not so great. What's the good news?'

'The good news is your figures are up.'

The listening figures for all radio in Northern Ireland are published every three months, so a relatively new presenter like Hugo would be eager, to the point of driving himself demented, to know how his show is performing.

'Well that's good to hear,' he said, wondering how on earth there could be any bad news to go with that. He was hardly going to get the sack if the numbers listening to the show were increasing. 'You said there was bad news as well?'

'Yes, let me hand you over to the boss.'

'Hugo, are you driving?' said Pat Loughrey. 'For if you are, you might want to pull over.'

'No problem, Pat.'

'Hugo, do you know anything about a tape of Irish songs that you recorded, probably about twenty years ago?'

There was no reply, only considerable banging and crashing, followed by some noises of pain in the background.

'I think he's crashed,' whispered Pat in a worried tone.

He hadn't. He'd pulled in to the side of the road and flung himself out the driver's door before he was sick over the car. 'As soon as he'd said the words,' Hugo says, 'I knew exactly what he was talking about.'

In 1979, mainly as a result of his drinking, Hugo's recording output had declined. So when he was asked to record an album of Irish songs, he jumped at the chance. These weren't songs like 'Carrickfergus' and 'The Hills of Donegal', they were more along the lines of 'Dublin in the Green' and 'Four Green Fields', but more fervent. With his usual couple of bottles of port for the throat beside him, Hugo had done the recording session in Monaghan, the compilation of rebel songs was released, he collected his money and went his sweet way.

Now, nearly twenty years later, a local politician had come into possession of one of the cassettes and wanted to know if the BBC knew anything about the matter and, more to the point, what they were going to do about it.

Austin Hunter, who was senior press officer for the BBC, established firstly that Hugo had no more surprise recordings in his back catalogue; next, the audience data was double-checked and it confirmed that, although people knew he was a Catholic, Hugo was not, and is not, perceived as belonging particularly to one side or another and that his listeners and viewers were drawn from all sections of the community.

Because of the incident's potential embarrassment to the BBC, the controller had informed management in London; their advice was unequivocal, Hugo should go. By this stage, Hugo had put his version of events to Pat and his senior colleagues in Belfast, and not a word of it differed from what had been reported; far from it, Hugo's story revealed more details of his circumstances at the time of the recording than anyone was aware of – the seriousness of his drinking, a career in freefall and an admission that he would have sold what self-respect he had left for any money.

Above all, from the outset, he was genuinely contrite. Throwing up over his car had only been a warm-up; Hugo apologised for bringing shame and disrespect to the BBC, to Pat, to his producers, to everyone who'd stood by him. He lamented the day he'd ever taken to the drink or, for that matter, set foot in Monaghan, and if there was any way to make up for the trouble he was causing, they had only to ask – he had the drawers of his desk already cleared.

His audience was stunned. Expecting to deal with an embarrassing but relatively straightforward enquiry, Austin and Pat realised they had a great story on their hands. Here was a soul in torment, a man who brought daily companionship to tens of thousands of people who was about to unravel because of a mistake he'd made years before.

Much more sensitive to the prevailing climate in Northern Ireland than his management colleagues in London, Pat told Hugo that he would stand by him, on one condition; Hugo had to agree to tell the full story to the press, hiding nothing and apologising openly.

Austin arranged an interview with Jim McDowell and Hugh Jordan of the *Sunday World* and Hugo delivered his story, including a list of every Orange hall he'd ever played in and every church social he'd attended, particularly Presbyterian. The story was published, warts and all. As expected, his listeners were moved. They wrote to Hugo expressing support, they telephoned the BBC to say what a fine man he was, and his listening figures continued to climb.

Hugo's recollection of that time is delivered wholeheartedly and with a shiver: 'You know the way people say that an icy hand clutches your stomach? Well, I know exactly how that feels.'

In any month, Hugo averages over one hundred thousand listeners to *Country Afternoon*. Some of them listen to the entire programme on several occasions a week; others dip in and out regularly; and some catch up from time to time. This is a high level of listening for an afternoon radio programme by any standard, yet the music is only one of the attractions; listeners are just as drawn to friendship, warmth, humour, banter, and perhaps above all, some sense of place, which is the bedrock of the programme. If it is true that no one living in an urban area of Northern Ireland is any more than four generations from their rural background, it may help explain why the composition of Hugo's radio audience confounds the expected patterns. There is a high level of listeners in the Greater Belfast area; the mix of class is greater than for other, more general, daily programmes; there is a higher than average number of young people listening; women, men, Catholics, Protestants, townies, culchies, even students find something in common, something to share. 'I met a woman recently who told me that her daughter had started university in England and that she missed her terribly,' says Hugo. 'The daughter would also get a bit homesick from time to time. When either of them is feeling low, they arrange to listen to the show – one at home on the radio in the kitchen, the other on her laptop – and they feel closer because they are sharing in the stories and banter. That is what it's all about.'

But Hugo doesn't please all of the people, all of the time. Among the texts and emails that expressed sympathy after he announced that he'd slipped on ice and had a seriously bruised hip was one that read: 'Pity Hugo hadn't fallen on his mouth and then we'd have been able to hear the records instead of him talking over the top of them or singing along.'

Hugo doesn't debate where he fits in the BBC – as far as he's concerned, that's for others to do. He takes the BBC's traditional motto at face value, that it is there to inform, educate and entertain, and entertainment is what he does. Whether it's with the afternoon country show; *Hugo and Friends* and *Town Challenge*; on television; *Children in Need*; or promoting the BBC's literacy and computer skills initiatives, what he does is what it promises in the *Radio Times*. He plays the best of country music, and in doing so, Hugo recognises and engages with an audience that wishes to engage with him in return, and he achieves this by using a language, an understanding of place, forty years of experience that tell him people want some light and lightness in their days, and a style of music that signals unequivocally what he's about.

So, what does the day job entail?

11

Remember, Your
Uncle Hugo Loves You

> Unless you're one of the top men in the BBC, you don't
> get an office. I don't care, at least I've got a desk;
> there's many a one has to share. I've a wee stereo
> system on the desk and a phone and a lamp. On top of
> one speaker there's a photo of my grandchildren and on
> top of the lamp sits my special 'Your Uncle Hugo Loves
> You' baseball hat. It's special, because if I wasn't doing
> what I'm doing, it wouldn't be there. Why would I want
> an office?

There are not many desks like Hugo Duncan's in the BBC. It bears
a fair resemblance to every house-proud woman's dream, and if Wee
Susie was to walk into the office area, she would probably be
satisfied with the tidiness and orderliness that was such a feature of
her own house in Townsend Street.

There's no clutter on the desk, not even a single yellow Post-it to
remind Hugo of some appointment. The computer keypad sits
parallel to the edge of the desk; the screen is set at a perfect forty-
five degree angle to the rectangular shape of the work area. Personal
mementoes are placed on the window ledge, on top of speaker
cabinets and at the corners of the desk. There are soft toys, framed
photos of his grandchildren, several ornamental clocks; if they're
ever moved during cleaning, Hugo replaces them with the precision
of a snooker referee setting the cue ball. Most of his male colleagues
regard this tidiness as verging on an obsession and not setting a
good example at all. The more eagle-eyed might notice that any

letter or note that requires attention is handed over to be dealt with by a member of the production team; it's easy to keep a tidy desk when someone else is in charge of the yellow stickies.

Over the back of his chair is a freshly ironed, short-sleeved, black shirt, for this is his working gear, and in the desk drawer is a wonderful array of aftershaves, body sprays and fresheners. He keeps two of everything just in case one should run out. Forty years on the road have taught Hugo that if he's prepared for anything, very little will surprise him.

Behind him are several tall cabinets stretching from ceiling to floor and packed with dozens of drawers containing CDs, laid out neatly and in perfect alphabetical order, from which the music for each day's programme is selected. One cabinet contains the American section – first on the list is Alabama and last is Faron Young. Another cabinet holds his collection of Irish country music, starting with Barbara Allen and ending with Sean Wilson. Yet another section holds his compilations of country, classics, and fifties and sixties material. As with his desk, Hugo knows exactly where everything is and the detail of the record catalogue is in his head, not in a reference book. The artist with the largest number of CDs is Garth Brooks, but among the most played is Brian Coll. This is not a scientific study, more a consensus of opinion of those who work on the programme. Among the few you might not expect to find in the *Country Afternoon* catalogue are the Beatles, Elvis Presley and Van Morrison, although those who know their country music history would argue that that is not a surprise, as all pop and rock music comes from country and country blues music in the first place.

There are no albums by Hugo Duncan, because he never plays his own recordings.

To the right of the desk is a small window that looks out onto Ormeau Avenue, with its constant flow of city-centre traffic. Directly across the street is the hotel occupying a site that was once a car park built on wasteland, before that, a linen mill and, before that, the Blackstaff River, once the filthiest stream flowing into the Lagan, which was eventually culverted by Victorian bricklayers and tilers. It's all a far cry from the hills of Tyrone and Donegal:

> Come down from the mountain, Katie Daly
> Come down from the mountain, Katie do,
> Come down from the mountain, Katie Daly
> We want to drink your good old mountain dew.

At the far end of Ormeau Avenue is the main Belfast station of the Northern Ireland Fire Brigade, so it's not unknown for Katie Daly to have the additional accompaniment of a fire engine siren or two when she's getting a blast on Hugo's CD player.

Other desks occupying this office advance in ranks of four. In the daytime, therefore, this is a busy, noisy area, with up to thirty people hot-desking and grabbing a seat where they can. Most of the staff who sit in this large, open-plan area work on music-based programmes, and Hugo works with the likes of John Bennett, Cherrie McIlwaine and Alan Simpson. So the odds are that at any time of the day there's music of some sort playing and, considering that Radio Ulster's young listeners' music strands – the noisy ones – are also based in this office, the mix of melodies can be a touch exotic. 'They play some stuff would make the old dog howl,' Hugo observes, 'but then, I suppose they say the same about the music I play.'

And the assortment of people is as rare as the music mix – young presenters, older broadcasters, producers, researchers – and the conversations and arguments range from football and Christmas shopping to the best place to stop for a cup of coffee on the road to Enniskillen. And there are benefits to being part of such an eclectic grouping, as Hugo recognises:

> Everybody has a view on everything, and if you want to
> find out something, you just stand up in your seat and

shout out the question. It would be a strange day that
the answer was long in coming back to you.

As well as folk scattered round the office, there's a constant stream
of visitors from other departments. They usually arrive on legitimate
business, though they're as likely to appear because they're on the
hunt for gossip. When Strabane was a much smaller town in Hugo's
youth, there wasn't much went on that somebody didn't know
something about. BBC departments have a very similar feel and
culture, which is one of the reasons he feels so at home there. He's
certainly regarded as a good and reliable contributor, not in the
slightest reluctant to give his point of view, even if he has no
experience of the matter under discussion.

On other occasions, visitors may be there because word has got
out that the second floor is a good spot for a quick snack. This
reputation goes back to the days when Hugo invited listeners to put
on the kettle and have afternoon tea with him. Being very fond of
a cream bun, he encouraged them to forget their diets and have a
cake or two along with their tea. Very soon, listeners began to send
him buns, éclairs, sponges, even big cakes, and if he stopped off for
petrol or called into a shop on his way to the studio, he was liable
to leave with yet more. Rather than waste such delights, they were
all spread out on the desks in the office and people from all over the
building got into the habit of calling for a bite of cake – accountants,
drivers, electricians, security men, even the odd member of Senior
Management from the Sixth Floor.

It's in such an environment that one of Northern Ireland's most
successful radio programmes goes about its daily business. 'I come
in here in the mornings about eleven o'clock,' says Hugo, 'and I
shout out, "Did you miss me?" And I get dog's abuse from every
corner of the office, young and old, tall, short, fat and skinny. It
makes me feel great.'

Directly opposite Hugo sit Joanne and Trish. They've been with him since his early days with the BBC in Belfast and understand the needs and expectations of his audience every bit as much as Hugo himself. One of the reasons for the continued success of his radio programmes on Radio Ulster and Radio Foyle is that the amount of tinkering with the product is kept to a minimum. Hugo's daily programme relies on a strong, direct link between himself and the listeners, a two-way link. Therefore it's important that those in the small team share a rare thing, they know who they're broadcasting to and why. It's natural, then, to assume that there's very little on which they would differ, but that's not always the case. For instance, Hugo picks the music under the watchful eye and ear of Joanne, for she knows he has his favourites and a typical exchange might go as follows:

'We'll play a bit of Dominic just after the news.'

'You played him yesterday.'

'No, I didn't, I said I would play him but I didn't put it in.'

'Believe me, you played Dominic Kirwan just before you did the Competition Teaser at half past two.'

'Away out of that.'

'Trish, didn't he play Dominic yesterday?'

'You did, Hugo. It was that song that Joe Dolan used to sing – you know the one.'

'"Good-looking Woman"?'

'That's it. Sure, you remember.'

'Maybe I did right enough. Youse know more about me than the angels in heaven.'

And, content in the knowledge that he's managed to stir it for a few moments, he turns around to continue burrowing away happily through his CD collection, and for anyone who cares to listen, he treats them to a short rendition of the chorus of Dolan's classic song:

> Oh me oh my you make me sigh
> You're such a good-looking woman

When people stop and people stare
You know it fills my heart with pride . . .

It's easy to suppose that all Hugo has to do is grab a handful of country music CDs and go to the studio and play them. No different from any other music broadcaster, however, he's keen to serve the music he loves as best he can. So he's always aware of the need for variation in tempo, style and subject. He says he doesn't even think consciously about these ingredients any more; they're just at the back of his mind when he's selecting any one of the three hundred or so music running orders he selects each year. He uses the same intuition built on experience that tells him what sort of crowd he has at one of his live gigs, what sort of mood they're in, and what will go down well with them:

> I'll be driving down the road listening to music and I'll
> hear a track and I think that would be great for just
> after the news at two o'clock and that sets me thinking
> to how a song from Philomena would sound good
> immediately after. These wee thoughts are running
> through my head all the time.

There are sad songs, uplifting songs, classics that have been recorded by a multitude of performers, and there are silly songs. Hugo and his team also know they have established his reputation as the one BBC broadcaster who is prepared to play the recordings of local country musicians and each day's music reflects the artists his listeners go to hear at the weekends, as well as those they might expect to hear at the Grand Ole Opry or watch on their YouTube collections.

One of Hugo's major frustrations is with people who dismiss his sort of music, his Irish country music, which is the butt of much humour, particularly its subject matter. This is often referred to as being about lost loves, missing your mother and losing your dog with a wee bit of gospel thrown in. He contends that, as much as any other genre of music and maybe more, the music and the words of Irish country reflect what people think about their own lives. That means there is sadness, yes, but there's also fun, there's life. 'My listeners don't want to hear an hour and a half of dirges,' he says, 'no more than I want to play them. What they do want is what they know, so I give them the fast tunes, the big hitters and the men and women from down the road who mean something to them.'

And no one is more ready than his listeners and the country music fans to remind him of this commitment to their music communities round the country, as Hugo recalls:

> I was in this shop one day and a nice wee woman about
> fifty shouted at me, 'Hey Hugo, come here till I speak to
> you', and I went over expecting her to give me big kiss
> and all and tell me I was great. Not a bit of her. She
> poked me in the stomach and she says, 'Jackie Nelson's
> had a new record out this last two weeks and I haven't
> heard sight nor sound of it on your show yet. Have the
> two of you fallen out?' What do you say? But I had
> Jackie in the running order for the next day's
> programme, I can tell you.

Perhaps it's because his own experiences weren't always happy and he knows that life isn't as straightforward as we'd wish it to be that Hugo always searches for the positive in his work and his music. He wants people around him to be happy, he wants his listeners to be happy, and he spends much of his time working out how to bring a bit of fun, a sense of lightness into their daily lives. So once the music has been sorted out for that day's programme, he turns to competitions, teasers, word games and logic puzzles, which he uses to challenge his on-air audience. But not before he's challenged and often tormented his office audience.

'Here's one for you' will be shouted from his small corner and a collective groan goes up from the rest of the poor folk trying to get on with their work. 'There's a field with cows and men in it. If there are twenty heads and seventy legs in the field, how many cows and how many men are in the field?'

No matter how hard his colleagues try to ignore it, they get sucked in, especially after the question has been repeated a couple of times and personal challenges thrown down.

'Come on, you've got a big university degree and you can't do an easy sum!'

If it's not a brain teaser, it's a nonsense riddle.

This can go on for thirty minutes or so, as Hugo rehearses the patter that will both perplex and entertain his audience from half past one until three o'clock. Knowing that he can so easily annoy those in the office delights him, especially as he knows also that they're secretly trying to work out the answers. This first half of the day is simply an essential, if enjoyable, part of the process that sets him up for what he calls the real deal – the crack of the afternoon's live broadcast. Later on air he will take equal pleasure from gleefully pointing out to various lorry drivers, digger operators and men in tractors that they're totally wrong and they'd be far better sticking to their day's work. The response to the teasers and wordplays is huge, yet it all came about by accident.

After it had owned up to fiddling the results of several high-profile competitions, the BBC banned competitions on all programmes. These, however, are a convenient way to encourage viewer and listener participation and on a show like Hugo's even a silly question with only an Uncle Hugo hat as a prize could keep the phones hopping for the afternoon. When he duly informed his audience that the competitions had stopped, about ten minutes later a man phoned the programme and said that the prizes didn't matter and he had a cryptic puzzle that he challenged Hugo and his listeners to solve. Unable to solve it himself, Hugo threw it open to his audience, the phones lit up, and now he runs two or three a day and his listeners can't get enough of them.

The *Radio Times* lists Hugo's show simply: 'Country Afternoon with Hugo Duncan – the best of country music. With news and travel at 2.00.' What it really is, is a daily assembly of people across Northern Ireland and beyond who have a culture that is partly defined by country music and who share a common regard for someone who has chosen to identify with that culture.

Hugo carries everything he needs for the programme to Studio 8A, all contained in a stout box with 'BBC' stencilled on the side. He is strangely fond of the box, because it's a form of status symbol, a reminder to him that he is part of this organisation that he's old enough to remember as an iconic brand. The box contains his CDs, letters, cards, any notes he needs, a pack of tissues, a few bars of chocolate and his emergency kit of half a dozen tins of Red Bull. By the time he has hoisted the black leather chair in the studio high enough to settle in behind the control desk, the first of that day's several hundred phone calls, emails and texts will be on their way to the programme, often before he has had a bit of banter with *Talkback* presenter David Dunseith and said good afternoon to the country.

These messages from the listeners form one of the vital cores of the programme's continued success. There are the usual dedications and requests; there are expressions of sympathy for others in trouble or those who are sick. There are congratulations on births, engage-ments and marriages, usually accompanied by free advice, not all of it repeatable on air. Often there are acknowledgements that some-one has done a kindness or is simply 'nice'. There are exhortations for people to get on with their work and stop idling, and there seems to be an endless stream of men with names like Volvo Vincent and Digger Boy Dave encouraging each other to 'horse it into them', 'flash the lights' and 'give her the gutty'. A stranger to this world would perhaps be justified in wondering what sort of society he'd wandered into and whether there was a quick way out. But if he listens on, he'll discover it is an assembly of warmth and shared values, with a mixture of banter and fun. It could never be classed as 'worthy' broadcasting, but its intent is serious and its impact is genuine because the audience regards *Country Afternoon* as their part of the BBC, and that is important for both them and the broadcaster.

Country Afternoon is also one of those programmes that divides the population; the tens of thousands who are regular listeners love it, but many others can't abide it, and sometimes Hugo feels that dislike at first hand.

> I was in a café one day, driving to the BBC, and this woman was talking to the man serving at the counter. He noticed me, for I called there most days, and he winked and asked her if she ever listened to Radio Ulster. She said she listened a lot and she listed all the programmes from *Good Morning Ulster* through to *Talkback*. She said she had trouble with Gerry (Anderson) but could stick him. I asked her if she didn't ever listen on beyond Dunseith and she said, 'Oh no. Do you see the man who comes on then? I think he's simple.' As we talked I could see her expression change as she realised gradually that I was that man, and I suppose I took a certain pleasure from the fact that she was embarrassed. I know she didn't mean it the way it maybe sounded but it was sore.

When Hugo was brought into the Radio Ulster schedule, his job was clear: 'Play country music, and make sure you mention all the local names, but don't talk a lot.' For in truth, Hugo was not a natural broadcaster, let alone interviewer. When he started in radio, he struggled for words and was uncertain of the right way to say things or, perhaps more fairly, he had not yet discovered his own way of saying those things and felt that there was a peculiar BBC way of talking to listeners that he would have to learn. Hugo recalls those early days:

> And then someone said it didn't really matter what the
> BBC thought, as long as the people they were paying me to
> talk to understood what I was saying. That's when I
> realised that I like people, I like talking about what they're
> up to, and I love having fun with them, so that's what I
> should do on air. And that's what I've done ever since.

And something special began to happen, because the audience targeted by his show knew that not only was this the same Hugo Duncan they'd danced to over the years, he was also on their side, and despite what others might say about their music and culture, Hugo remained happy to stand by them. A language evolved through the messages and the shared identities. Even though the accents differ, the use of grammar fluctuates and the expressions vary in sophistication, those who use the language recognise each other through Hugo. In straightforward terms, they understand what they're talking about, have plenty to say, and contact the programme in their hundreds every day of the week.

This is what keeps his fans faithful. Hugo is honest in his broadcasting; he doesn't try to do things he knows he can't do; he doesn't try to be smarter than he really is – which is pretty smart. So the texts and emails become links to regular contributors to the programme; they usher in those who only contact him when they have an occasion to mark; they reflect the life and wit of listeners from Belfast to Belleek, Articlave to Armagh. And most of this dialogue is upbeat, vibrant, positive, and often funny. Like one punter's request: 'Hugo, say hello to the wife; it's her birthday. She's the quietest woman I know, talks in whispers. She should have been a telephonist.'

For others, his company is simply enough. 'I met a man one day who was undergoing chemotherapy treatment for a tumour,' Hugo recalls. 'I asked him how he was doing and he told me he was going through hell but that he was still alive and he listened to the show every day because it made him smile and gave him a lift.'

The operation of the afternoon programme is straightforward enough. Hugo holds court in the studio, sympathising with those for whom life has taken a downturn, slagging and cheerfully insulting those who are clearly in much more robust form, knowing that they'll give as good as they get. Meanwhile, the 'girls', as he calls them, run in and out with messages, while even more are typed onto the constantly updated screen that hangs over his studio desk.

Every what's-on is read out, no matter the event, for in small communities recognition from elsewhere can be enough to bring that extra few people through the door. On the run-up to the three o'clock news when his show ends, he starts to invite votes for that day's cult song, with which he will finish the programme. What started out as a specially composed song, 'Your Uncle Hugo Loves You', led to others writing in similar vein and there are now enough songs to make a chart of their own, including 'I'll Make Love to You in the Henhouse if You'll Only Egg Me On', 'Flash Your Lights at Me', and the king or queen of them all, 'Horse It into Ya, Cynthia'. 'Cynthia' has achieved a mythical reputation ever since BBC Radio 1 presenter Scott Mills, who was broadcasting his afternoon show from the studio next door to Hugo's, observed in awe to his nationwide audience: 'There's a guy here called Hugo and every day at the same time he plays this record, "Horse It into Ya, Cynthia". You have no idea the response he gets from his listeners. Makes you wonder what playlists are all about.'

Then comes the Benny Hill music, final goodbyes and the bit the listeners know off by heart: 'Thanks to Trish Coyle from the banks of the Foyle and the Wee Woman with the Big Stick, Joanne Murphy. Thanks to you, and remember, your Uncle Hugo loves you.'

Easy? Perhaps. But as Dolly Parton might say, 'It takes a lot of thought to make it sound as if you've just thought of it.'

12

That's Me, On the TV

Hugo's years with the BBC have been very good to him. Many radio presenters do just that, present radio programmes and rarely, if ever, do any television work. Along with George Jones, Hugo was co-presenter of *Town Challenge*, which ran to five series during the nineties, and he was the host of *Hugo and Friends*, which lasted for four seasons.

Town Challenge was filmed on location in towns and villages across Northern Ireland and its main purpose was to show as much of the landscape and scenery as possible, while cramming as many local faces and voices as possible into each programme. George and Hugo each took charge of a team and tried to guide them to victory via a series of challenges, games and tasks. Each season culminated in a grand finale, at which one of the twenty or so teams would be crowned Top Town. '*Town Challenge* was very good to me,' says Hugo; 'it got my face known way beyond the circles of the country music and, apart from anything else, it was great fun to do.'

Hugo enjoys everything about the process of television – he loves the cameras, he doesn't find rehearsal boring and he gets on famously with the hordes of technical staff involved in the production of a multi-camera recording, especially the riggers. These are the men with muscles who lug the gear around – boxes of equipment, miles of cable, bits of cameras – and then drive the trucks home at the end of the day. They are the first to arrive and the last to leave; they work hard and have a lot of hanging around to do while the creative types create. They have seen it all, many times over, and for all his inexperience, they were on Hugo's side, which he found hugely supportive. 'Campbell, Shane, big Hughie –

I had great banter with them all,' he recalls. 'When things were going wrong, if I was making mistakes, which I did all the time, they just laughed or shrugged their shoulders and we got on with it. They kept me relaxed.'

Certainly Hugo did make mistakes. With no television presenting experience, he had to learn the craft as each *Town Challenge* programme was being made. One major problem was that he has difficulty reading a script. This problem had first arisen when he began his Radio Foyle work. Because he was so inexperienced, Mickey Bradley had suggested he write his short links between the records he was introducing, but Hugo found it difficult to sound in any way natural. Reading and narrating the links at the same time didn't come easily to him. This is partly because he never reads; he never had the time. As he acknowledges himself, he was travelling, playing or drinking and has never in his fifty-plus years read for pleasure. As a result, words frighten him. That creates a bit of a problem in television, where so much of the flow of the operation revolves round the script.

On *Town Challenge*, the links were written on big cards that were held up beside the camera. They'd start off with about ten cards; all he had to do was read each one as it replaced the one before, but he struggled to get the correct phrasing. The number of cards would be reduced until he was barely reading a couple of sentences. To paraphrase Eric Morecambe, all the right words were there but not necessarily in the right order, and they certainly didn't trip off his tongue easily. Not only did he feel a fool, he knew that his performance was being talked about by some on the production team. 'I wasn't supposed to hear,' says Hugo, 'but there were times I overheard them asking on the talkback whether I couldn't see the cards or not, and then wondering if I could read big words. The more I tried, the worse it got, and then sometimes they wondered aloud, was I too stupid or what? I've seen me drive home after a day's filming with tears in my eyes because what they were saying was so personal.'

But he persevered. The links were only a small part of the programme, much of the rest of the content required Hugo to do what he does best – have fun with the people. On the plus side was the fact that he was clearly becoming known as a television entertainer as well as a country singer. Halfway through the first series of *Town Challenge* he was in Bundoran delivering some publicity posters for his forthcoming summer tour. Being the holiday season, the town was busy and he was astonished to hear groups of young teenage girls shouting his name, until he realised that they knew him, not from his music, but from his new role in television.

Dressing up was an important part of being a presenter of *Town Challenge*, and George and Hugo appeared in many guises. Hugo once spent a day in Markethill, County Armagh, dressed as a duck, and both men participated in all sorts of silly games, got soaked, were gunged, and acted as moving targets at which competitors could hurl missiles, the messier the better. The crowds who attended the location recordings were enormous. Hugo was well used to being the centre of attention, but for the first time he was meeting people who hadn't turned up just because of him. Many came along because they knew George from his years in the entertainment and broadcasting business; many others came because their local town and people were involved and there was always the chance that they might get themselves on the box.

So there were those in attendance who weren't by any means fans of the music that Hugo played and were quite happy to slag off both him and the music, something he didn't mind at all. Indeed, he was happy to engage in the banter. What pleased him was that people were happy to engage with him, whether they liked his music or not. 'It demonstrated again to me that there are no barriers,' he says. 'People think that I'm approachable, that I won't turn my back on them.'

Hugo also drew support from them. During the time he was having his difficulties with reading the script, he took great delight one day in chatting to a man who was leaning against one of the outside broadcast vehicles. 'Isn't it great to have the gift of the gab?' the man observed. It was meant as a compliment and Hugo took it as such, for he knows that 'having the gift of the gab' isn't the same as being able to blether or just prattle on; the phrase implies that the listener can engage with the speaker, that there's communication and understanding. As long as Hugo is convinced that that is taking place, he's happy.

Town Challenge brought him some of his lightest moments on television and some of the dullest. He always enjoyed the games, leading a town team, encouraging them, going through the same challenges, suffering the same ignominies, mixing with the local folk and generally getting stuck in. The show became less fun to do when the focus shifted more on to competition and away from participation, when the presenters introduced items or sections rather than joined in. Recording the treasure hunts, where each team had to solve clues about the surrounding area, was the hard work. George would go off with one team for a day's filming and Hugo would go off with the other. Most of the time was spent travelling from one location to the next or hanging around waiting for the clues to be set up and the sequences rehearsed. What he found most frustrating about these days was that he had very little to do, and that simply has never suited him:

What made it worse was you'd spend all day out and about and it would end up as a couple of minutes maximum in the finished show. I always felt as if I was wasting time. But the outside broadcasts themselves made up for that. George and I would get supporters of the two teams whipped up, we'd let them off the leash and away we'd go. In the rain, it was torture; in the sun, it wasn't work at all.

One of the last recordings of the 1998 series brought home graphically the fact that tragedy can strike at any moment and just because you're an entertainer doesn't mean you don't have difficult tasks to do and circumstances to deal with. The venue was Ardglass, County Down, and in the crowd were quite a number who had travelled from Irvinestown, for that town's team was in with a strong chance of making it through to the final. Reports began to come through that a large bomb had exploded somewhere in the west and the initial understanding was that it might have been Irvinestown. This was known only to the production team and the presenters, who, while considering what to do since there were the people from the town in the audience, were then informed that the explosion had taken place in Omagh.

By the time the news became public, the outside broadcast recording was coming to an end and Hugo headed for Belfast, having arranged to present his regular Saturday night programme from the radio studios in Ormeau Avenue. By the time he arrived there, the full scale of the tragedy and devastation was known. The awful loss of life stunned and shocked the country, and those with family, friends and acquaintances in that community were desperately trying to find out who had been killed and injured.

Hugo has lived twenty miles down the road from Omagh all his life, has friends there and some of Joan's family live in the town; he does business locally and he laughs and sings and jokes with its people. And on 15 August he went on air not knowing if some of those he knew were among the dead and injured. He remembers that awful day:

> Anna, who was head of broadcast, stayed around the
> studio that evening and we had decided that the lines
> should be open for listeners to express their feelings. I
> don't know what I said or what I did. There were
> hundreds and hundreds of messages from listeners. This

was a country music show and the people in Omagh are
great supporters of country music; I had sung for them,
yet what could you say? I never had to do a harder
broadcast in my life.

He was drained when he finished the broadcast and all he wanted
to do was get home and start talking to Joan, to friends, to start
ringing around. But he had a concert date in Derrygonnelly, County
Fermanagh, where, like all those attending, he tried to take in and
cope with the horror of the day.

Some weeks after his broadcast that Saturday night, Hugo
received a note from a listener that said simply, 'I cried all night; not
even you could bring a smile to my face, but I knew you were there.'
Throughout the many years of violence, listeners turned to their
radio stations, not only for news, but also for companionship, for
some sense of normality, some reminder that although there was
trouble, they could cope, and that there was always someone to talk
to. Hugo was one of those they turned to.

Town Challenge may have been the show that brought Hugo his
first sustained television work but it was *Hugo and Friends* that was
closest to his heart. Once it became clear that he was attracting
large audiences to the afternoon radio strand, the schedulers were
looking for a way to maximise the brand that had been created and
Hugo and Friends was the project that was planned to deliver that
same relationship to BBC Northern Ireland television. It trod the
path taken by *Make Mine Country*, a television series from the
eighties on which he had been a guest. Hugo's new series, however,
placed a greater emphasis on local talent, much in keeping with his
strategy for the daily radio programme. Different series were filmed
in a variety of venues but it was at its most enjoyable in Belfast's
Grand Opera House, which lent the show the theatrical style of
Nashville's Grand Ole Opry and, in fact, was given that title for the
duration of the series.

Although it was producer Fedelma Harkin who devised the series, Hugo also believed there was a need for such a show, because it had been some years since *Make Mine Country* was broadcast. 'I loved having the names on,' he recalls; 'the likes of Crystal Gayle and Charley Pride, but what really delighted me was that I could give Irish singers the opportunity to be on TV in the North, especially the younger ones. But there were also others that I had looked up to and admired for years and here I was introducing them.'

Brian Coll and Philomena Begley, both legends and friends of Hugo's, shared the stage with him. One of his favourite press photos from the series is of Philomena in a black dress, with her glistening jewellery matched by the sparkle that's always in her eyes, Brian dressed in his emerald green rhinestone jacket with bola tie, and, in the middle with his arms round them, a beaming Hugo dressed in his customary black. Three friends sharing time together and sharing a few years as well.

Brendan Quinn, Susan McCann, Dominic Kirwan, Michael English, Declan Nerney and Louise Morrissey were among those on Hugo's guest list and he's pleased that he had some hand in boosting the careers of less well-known singers, like Mike Denver and Jimmy Buckley. 'All I know is how useful getting some television exposure was to me, both when I was starting out and then when I was trying to get it together again,' he says. 'What I was hoping to do was to put a wee bit back into the business that I love.'

As with *Town Challenge*, he was learning as he went along, and he encountered similar difficulties with the script. For this series, he was expected to use an autocue, a system that's perfect for a stage show such as the Opera House, for it allows the presenter to read the script displayed in the broad lens of the camera that he's addressing and it moves slowly up the screen to match his speed of delivery. To get around the problem, Hugo's producer would talk him through what was required, who was on next, where they were from and what they were going to perform, and he could deliver the information as if he were reading it. This solution was spot on, because that was how he had played his role as a front man for forty years. At a dance or a concert in the midst of the noise and bustle, people shout things in his ear about someone's anniversary or birthday, the number of years, the names, where they're from, and he has to make it a special moment, their special moment. The effect is spoiled somewhat if he introduces the anniversary waltz for Jimmy and Annie when it should be Winnie and Danny; so he has trained himself over the years to get it right.

As a novice television presenter, there was something else he didn't know. He didn't know to keep going until someone says stop, a lesson he learned the hard way.

It was final rehearsals for one of the shows from the Opera House and he was singing. Suddenly the PA system for the theatre audience failed and Hugo stopped mid-song. Fedelma blistered the talkback into his ear: 'When I say start, you start and you don't stop till I say stop, and when I say stop, you stop.' Hugo appreciated her directness:

> Now I didn't mind that, because she made sure I knew.
> She told it straight to my face, or to my ear, not behind
> my back, and then she came out on stage immediately
> after to say the rehearsal had gone well, and was I happy.
> She read me better than some others, and at the end of
> the day, what she was telling me was for my own sake.

All the recordings were made as though they were going out live, which meant that the show didn't stop unless there was a serious mistake. The adrenalin rush, then, for all concerned, was almost the same as for a completely live broadcast. Hugo would stand in the wings, feeling good in his black suit, microphone in hand and ready to enjoy what was undoubtedly one of the greatest highs of his musical career, the moment when the announcer's voice echoed around that fabulous entertainment venue: 'Ladies and gentlemen, please welcome your host, the Wee Man from Strabane, Hugo Duncan!' The lights would come up, the applause would lift, the band would hit the introduction to the Buck Owens classic 'Think of Me When You're Lonely', and Hugo would stride on to the stage. 'The one thought always went through my mind as I stepped out of the wings: if I die now, I die happy,' he says. And then he'd hit centre stage and within seconds he'd be in full flow, waving to friends in the stalls, rocking from side to side, doing what he does best:

> Think of me when you're lonely
> Think of me when you're blue
> Think of me when you're far away
> For I'll be thinking of you.

Working in broadcasting has not only allowed Hugo to give fellow musicians opportunities to perform and raise their profile, it has also given him the chance to have experiences and meet musicians who, had he remained only a singer, would have been unlikely to come his way.

He's made several trips to Nashville, for both radio and television projects, and has worked with some of the greatest names in the country music business – Lee Ann Womack, Skeeter Davis, Garth Brooks, Porter Wagoner and Ricky Skaggs, among others.

One visit that he found most moving was to the RCA Victor record label's Studio B in Nashville, when he stood on the spot where musical giants such as Elvis Presley, Jim Reeves, the Everly Brothers, Hank Locklin, Willie Nelson and Chet Atkins had recorded some of the most famous and best-loved songs in country music. Not only was he standing on the spot, he was in the company of Boots Randolph, a legendary Nashville session musician who had played with Elvis, Brenda Lee, Jerry Lee Lewis and Roy Orbison. Boots was regarded as the finest saxophone player in the session business and he was one of the musicians responsible for creating what became known as the Nashville sound, which can be heard on thousands of recordings issued from the late fifties through to the eighties.

But Hugo had another reason for meeting up with Boots. In 1963, Boots had a major hit with an instrumental called 'Yakety Sax', and this is the music that plays out the end of Hugo's radio programme every day of the week. He spent the afternoon filming with Boots but the footage has never been seen. When the programmes were edited back home in Belfast, there was just too much material and some had to go. Boots died in 2007 at the age of eighty and somewhere in a drawer or a cabinet in Broadcasting House there is a filmed conversation between Hugo and Boots about what it was like to play with Elvis.

One of the programmes that was broadcast reflected yet another memorable chapter in Hugo's career. He spent several days in the company of Tom T. Hall, who is regarded as one of the great writers of storytelling songs. Some of those artists for whom he wrote include Johnny Cash, Loretta Lynn and Waylon Jennings, and his most famous cross-over success was 'Harper Valley PTA', the song that Jeannie C. Riley took into the British charts in 1968. Hugo and Tom were filmed at Tom's house and in his recording studio, talking about the songs and about country music, and Hugo recorded some of his favourites as their composer looked on.

'Tom T. Hall is a songwriters' writer,' says Hugo. 'The respect in which he's held is awesome and I just felt so privileged that a man who has written one of my favourite songs of all time should be so willing and generous to spend his time with me.' That song is 'Old Dogs, Children and Watermelon Wine', written from the perspective of an old black man looking back on his long years and wondering what he has learned. 'I think it is one of the best examples of the story songs that Tom writes and it is a wonderful country song. Its subject is simple but honest and it makes you wonder about why the world can't be that way, which is what a lot of country songs do,' Hugo adds. His favourite lines perhaps come as no surprise, considering the troubles of the country and the town in which he has lived all his years, and they perhaps also reflect something of the personal troubles he's experienced in his life:

Old dogs care about you, even when you make mistakes
God bless little children while they're still too young to hate.
. . . .
Ain't but three things in this world that's worth a solitary dime
But old dogs and children and watermelon wine.

Because Hugo takes time to listen to people, because he's quick to offer his help, and because he knows how much people want to be remembered by those they've met, he looks for those same qualities in the folk that he meets. When he returned to Nashville several years later, he put in a call to Tom, hoping that he hadn't forgotten their acquaintance and that they might get a chance to meet up again. The response was all he could have hoped for: 'I'm retired now,' said Tom, 'but when I heard that Hugo was in town, I said to myself, he did me no harm the last time he was here and I reckon he'll do me no harm this time.' It's a line Hugo treasures.

Another of the treasures is the meeting with Garth Brooks, but this one Hugo remembers because of what it so nearly wasn't. Hugo was due to visit the Grand Ole Opry to celebrate its eightieth anniversary and for months before the event Joanne and Trish had been trying to set up an interview with the singer. Trish had remained in the office till eight or nine o'clock on many evenings to make those transatlantic calls, working her way through the list of contacts and moving from one member of Garth's entourage to the next. Performers such as Garth are much sought after and legions of people are employed to look after their various interests, so any request for access has to be written down in triplicate and passed over countless desks until someone gives it the thumbs up, or down.

Eventually someone must have told Garth just how big Hugo was in Ireland, for permission was given for the interview to take place, but strict guidelines were imposed. Hugo alone would be allowed to meet the singer. He would be permitted one question only and that was to be about the Grand Ole Opry, not about Garth. Apart from being granted an interview, one of the few positive aspects of the affair was that, as a result of the endless phone calls and organisational hassles, Hugo's team was on first-name terms with one of Garth's people, a publicist, Nancy, who exercised some influence.

The meeting was due to take place backstage in the theatre and it was here that they met Darlene, a Southern lady who was a PR representative for the Opry. Darlene was determined to be as obstructive and uncooperative as possible. First, she tried to turn them away. Then she said that only Hugo could go behind the scenes to meet Garth. This presented a small technical difficulty because Hugo had no idea how to operate the tape recorder. As it became clear that Darlene was not for turning, Joanne gave him a crash course on which buttons to push just before he was due to put the one question to one of the biggest names in country music. And then Joanne was shown the door by Darlene, at which point Hugo's blood pressure probably went over any sensible limit – he likes his troops round him.

At this juncture, Nancy appeared on the scene to collect them and immediately demanded to know where the two Irish girls were. She proceeded to tear Darlene to shreds, collected Joanne and Trish, and led them all off to meet the great man.

Hugo didn't hold out much prospect of there being much crack in store, especially when he heard Garth say to Nancy, 'Does Hugo know about the one question?'

'Yes, he does.'

'And does he know it's to be about the Opry?'

'Sure does, Garth.'

'Show him in then.'

The room was tiny. When Hugo and his team had squeezed in, Garth greeted them all, found them chairs, and then proceeded to chat away happily for the next thirty minutes about the Opry, his favourite songs, his family, and Ireland, as if there had never been any conditions attached to the meeting. 'We were sitting so close our knees were interlocked and he was about six inches from my face and it was like we were just in someone's front room,' says Hugo. 'I couldn't remember what we talked about till I listened to the tape.' It was fortunate that Garth didn't stick to the rules, because by the time Hugo had been ushered in, he had forgotten the one question he was supposed to ask.

Making a Difference was a major community project that the BBC in Northern Ireland produced for a number of years. Its prime purpose was to acknowledge the unsung contributions made by ordinary folk to the lives of their family, friends and neighbours. Each year its climax was a gala entertainment night hosted by BBC television in the Grand Opera House. The A to Z indexes of entertainers in Britain, Ireland and the States were scoured to find names prepared to come and support the cause. Word must have travelled as far as Greece, for Nana Mouskouri showed up one year. In its second year, 2000, word came back that Charley Pride would be happy to appear for the price of a couple of first-class transatlantic air fares and a day or two in Ireland to visit old friends.

Estimates of Charley's record sales sit at around seventy million, so when Hugo, who was already on the bill, was asked if he'd look after Charley at the grand finale on the night, guide him to his spot on stage, and make sure he stuck by him, he needed no second bidding. They were introduced at rehearsals, the tall, black, country singer, born on a cotton farm, shaking hands with the Wee Man from Strabane, and Charley pronouncing Hugo's name in his characteristic Southern drawl that seemed to add about three extra syllables.

That night Charley sang 'Kiss an Angel Good Morning'. Hugo can't remember what he sang, being there was enough. 'I had been playing this man's music since I had the old eight-track stereo in the car and here he was, standing beside me on the stage of the Grand Opera House, on TV for everyone to see,' he says, still glowing from the memory of that evening.

In the Europa Hotel after the show, Hugo and Charley chatted at length about their shared love of music, their different backgrounds and their families. All those who met Charley on that trip agree with Hugo's observation that no one ever got the impression that Charley wasn't interested, that time was pressing, or that at any moment he would turn and walk away. It's interesting that Hugo should set so much store by this, for he creates exactly the same impression when he's dealing with people, whether they are young singers, old friends or members of the public. Charley was also enormous fun; he followed his own adage to the letter – music is serious but don't be too serious. Charley returned to Belfast several years later to appear in *Hugo and Friends*. During rehearsals, Hugo, Charley, Brendan Quinn and the band got so engrossed in the shared joy of a jamming session that the producer's cries for them to stop were repeatedly ignored. Hugo clearly hadn't taken the producer's earlier lesson as much to heart as he'd claimed.

At home, in the front hall of Hugo's house in Strabane, hangs one of Hugo's prized possessions – a large photo of Charley, wearing the lord mayor of Belfast's chain of office, and Hugo with his arms around him.

The programme that Hugo remembers best from all the series of *Hugo and Friends* is the special they did with the Bellamy Brothers. Again, he singles it out because it included so many friends, the music was great, and they all had enormous fun. The Bellamys accepted a challenge to write a spoof version of their signature hit

'If I Said You Had a Beautiful Body', which went along the lines of 'If you said I had a beautiful body / I would hold it against you . . .'

And they also sang a storming version of 'Red Neck Girl'. Brendan Quinn and Hugo entertained their guests during rehearsals with tales of how the two of them used to hold car races on the roads out of Dublin. And the Queen of Country, Philomena, still able to fit into stage outfits that were designed for her quite a few years ago, treated the brothers to a wonderful version of their own song that targets the lost generation that came home from Vietnam, 'Old Hippie'. A highlight of the show was the Hughes Brothers from Monaghan, who tackled another Bellamy Brothers song, 'Shine Them Buckles'.

Hugo remembers that evening fondly:

> It was one of those great nights. John Reid was Secretary of State and he was in the audience. He's a great country fan. He'd sit and chat for ages about his favourite singers, and he used to listen to the radio show. He plays a bit as well. He always threatened to come in and play on the show but we never got round to it. He must have had other things to do.

Among other memorable television moments was the Patrick Kielty pilot for a new series which proposed a regular slot for the Rickety Wheel. A music-hall device that's been around for many years, its purpose in this show was to match celebrities up to an inappropriate song, which they then had to perform. What the producers needed was someone who was a bit of crack, who wouldn't mind being made fun of, and who wouldn't be offended if his contribution was never seen by the wider audience.

Hugo was their man. The audience consisted of Queen's University students prised away from their studies with promises of a glass or two of BBC wine. To a man and a woman, they took Hugo to their hearts. As they chanted his name with all the enthusiasm of a full house at Liverpool's Kop at Anfield, 'Hugh-Goooo, Hugh-Goooo', Patrick spun the big, very rickety wheel and the brake was eventually put on when the arrow pointed to 'Teenage Kicks' by the Undertones. A roar went up that would have done credit to a crowd scene in *Gladiator*. Cormac O'Kane's band launched into the instantly recognisable opening chords and Hugo gave it everything he'd got. His performance was brilliant. The crowd stood, they clapped along, they shouted, they sang, and Patrick was in the midst of it all, conducting the entire studio. When the song finished, the applause was deafening. Kielty got the series and Hugo was one of the first guests on the new show.

The extraordinary coincidences that occurred in the course of that recording simply demonstrate what a small part of the world it is that we live in. Jack Kielty, Patrick's father, had been one of Hugo's managers and Hugo has known the family for many years. The bass player in the Undertones, whose song had been picked for him to sing, Mickey Bradley, had been Hugo's first producer at Radio Foyle, the one who told him he wasn't there because he was a broadcaster, he was there because he was Hugo Duncan. And Hugo's recollection of that occasion? 'It was the most frightening thing I ever did and one of the most wonderful. I have never experienced anything like the energy that flowed into me in that studio.'

Being an Undertone one moment, wandering around Markethill dressed as a duck the next; life doesn't really come any more varied and enjoyable. So if Hugo is asked to reflect on his four series of *Hugo and Friends*, seemingly endless editions of *Town Challenge*, American specials in Nashville, *Children in Need*, guest appearances on *Kielty* and *Give My Head Peace*, and his personal guide to his early years in Strabane in the *Music Asides* series, he'll complain that his face doesn't fit any more on television, but happily joke that it still fits on radio, where he manages to pack in over three hundred and fifty hours of broadcasting and forty outside broadcasts a year. Listeners and fans contact him via many thousands of emails, texts and letters, singing his praises, wishing him well, thanking him for his kindnesses. If that doesn't cheer him up, he can always get out the video recorder and watch the old tapes.

It will be some time yet before Hugo has time to put his feet up and watch old tapes of *Town Challenge* or *Hugo and Friends*. Rarely does he have a weekend when he's not playing a couple of dates and the last weekend of March 2008 is typical. Having just celebrated his fifty-eighth birthday, he has taken a rare day off from his radio show, not to relax and take a bit of time to himself – that would be decidedly out of character. Hugo has asked for leave on the Friday so that he can accommodate a quick weekend tour of Scotland and the extra day means that he will be able to squeeze in four performances on the trip.

The whirlwind visit will take him from Glasgow to Dundee and back again via Stirling, with a final gig on the Sunday night before he heads to Stranraer to catch the morning ferry. These days, Hugo turns up and a band will be there waiting for him. On a series of dates like this, the musicians are usually hired in, so all he has to do is drive himself from venue to venue, and a few more hundred miles will make little difference to the eighty thousand or so that he will cover during the course of the year.

He has chosen the black BMW 4 x 4 for this trip, and not just because it allows him a better view of the countryside. Hugo's doing the driving but sharing the car with Frankie McBride, the man whose shoes he stepped into nearly forty years ago when the Polka Dots became the Tall Men.

As the two old acquaintances travel the roads of Scotland, Hugo tells Frankie about the book that's being written about his life and they start to swap stories about places they have played and people they've met. They try to work out the number of venues they've worked in and the miles they've covered. Frankie has a stab at how often he's sung 'Five Little Fingers', and although he reckons it's well more than Hugo has sung 'Brady from Strabane', the attempt to work out each sum ends in laughter and head-shaking as they lose themselves in hundreds of thousands of miles and enough concert halls, dance halls and cabaret lounges to fill a telephone book.

One weekend of music and reminiscence later, Hugo catches the 04.55 ferry on Monday morning from Stranraer, has his breakfast on the boat, and after docking in Belfast, drives to his home in Strabane to have a shower. He plays with his grandchildren, asks his daughter if there's anything she needs, gathers up a couple of the carefully ironed, short-sleeved black shirts that Joan always has ready for him, and by ten o'clock the Wee Man from Strabane is on the road again, heading back to Belfast and the BBC to present his first show of the week.

And, once again, it's only Monday.